# ABSOLUTELY EVERYTHING
# YOU NEED TO KNOW

**Written by**
Steve Pantaleo and Dean Miller

# CONTENTS

**01: MEET THE ICONS** 4
André the Giant 6
Bruno Sammartino 8
Hulk Hogan 10
Shawn Michaels 12
Ric Flair 14
Trish Stratus 16
Ultimate Warrior 18
Stone Cold Steve Austin 20
Randy Savage 22
Sting 24
The Rock 26
Bret "Hit Man" Hart 28
WWE Hall of Fame 30

**02: SUPERSTARS OF TODAY** 32
John Cena 34
Randy Orton 36
Undertaker 38
Brock Lesnar 40
AJ Styles 42
Triple H 44
The McMahon Family 46
General Managers 48
Seth Rollins 50
Dean Ambrose 52
Roman Reigns 54
Chris Jericho 56
Kevin Owens 58
Charlotte 60
Sheamus 62
The Miz 64
Big Show 66
Dolph Ziggler 68
Sasha Banks 70
Scary Superstars 72
Becky Lynch 74
*RAW* Superstars 76

*SmackDown Live* Standouts 78
Superstar Managers 80
Cruiserweights 82

**03: CHAMPIONSHIPS** 84
WWE Championship 86
Intercontinental Championship 88
Women's Championship 90
WWE Universal Championship 92
United States Championship 94
Tag Team Championship 96
*King of the Ring* 98
Retired Championships 100

**04: FACTIONS, STABLES, & TAG TEAMS** 102
The New Day 104
D-Generation X 106
The Usos 108
The New World Order 110
The Four Horsemen 112
The Dudley Boyz 114
The Legion of Doom 116
Edge and Christian 118
The Heenan Family 120
*RAW* Tag Teams 122
*SmackDown* Tag Teams 124
Legendary Tag Teams 126
The Authority 128
Announcing Teams 130

**05: BIG EVENTS** 132
*RAW* Facts 134
*Royal Rumble* 136
*WrestleMania* 138
*Money in the Bank* 140
No Escape and No Relief 142
*Starrcade* 144
*SummerSlam* 146

*SmackDown Live* 148
*Extreme Rules* 150
*Survivor Series* 152
WCW and the Monday Night Wars 154
ECW and the Brand's Revival 156

**06: SUPERSTARS OF TOMORROW** 158
NXT: The Future of WWE 160
Performance Center 162
*NXT TakeOver* Specials 164
The NXT Championship 166
The NXT Women's Championship 168
The NXT Tag Team Championship 170
The Dusty Classic 172
The WWE Draft 174

**07: WWE BEYOND THE RING** 176
WWE History 178
WWE Network 180
WWE Studios 182
WWE in the Community 184
*Total Divas* 186
Licensing and Merchandise 188
Finding the Next Superstars 190
Touring the World 192
The WWE Universe 194

Glossary 196
Index 198
Acknowledgments 200

Shawn Michaels descends from the sky to challenge Undertaker at *WrestleMania 25*.

# 01

## MEET THE ICONS

Shawn Michaels leaps from the top rope before he defeats Chris Jericho at *WrestleMania XIX* in March 2003.

## A SHOW OF GIANTS

Size has always mattered in sports entertainment, with everyone trying to measure up to the enormous André the Giant—who even managed to tower over massive Superstars like Undertaker and Big Show.

### SIZE CHART

**UNDERTAKER**
6ft 10in (2.08m)

**BIG SHOW**
7ft (2.13m)

**ANDRÉ THE GIANT**
7ft 4in (2.24m)

Jake "The Snake" Roberts was a longtime rival of André the Giant, and André would use his size advantage to punish The Snake as much as possible.

### INFOMANIA

**DATE OF BIRTH:** May 19, 1946

**HEIGHT:** 7ft 4in (2.24m)

**WEIGHT:** 520lbs (240kg)

**HOMETOWN:** Grenoble, France

**SIGNATURE MOVE:** Sitdown Splash—André dropped his massive frame on the chest of a downed opponent.

**DEBUT:** André defeated Buddy Wolfe on March 26, 1973 in Madison Square Garden, New York City.

**RETIRED:** André's last major appearance for WWE was at *SummerSlam 1991*, in a tag team with the Bushwackers.

## Q: WHICH NOBEL PRIZE WINNER USED TO DRIVE ANDRÉ THE GIANT TO SCHOOL?

**A:** Samuel Beckett. As a child, André was unable to fit on the school bus, so the playwright, who was a neighbor and family friend, drove the young André to school in his truck.

**FOR MORE THAN** two decades, no one loomed larger over the world of sports entertainment than André the Giant. At 7ft 4in (2.24m) and 520lbs (240kg), he was the biggest competitor in WWE. The Eighth Wonder of the World was inducted into the WWE Hall of Fame in 1993.

## "IT'S NOT MY FAULT, BEING THE BIGGEST AND THE STRONGEST."

ANDRÉ THE GIANT

### TITLE TRIVIA

André the Giant teamed with Haku to form the Colossal Connection tag team. Together, they beat Demolition for the World Tag Team Championship on December 30, 1989.

## IN DETAIL

### ANDRÉ THE GIANT VS. HULK HOGAN, *THE MAIN EVENT* (FEBRUARY 5, 1988)

Almost a year after failing to win the WWE Title against Hulk Hogan at *WrestleMania III*, André earned another shot at the Championship on *The Main Event*. In his most controversial win, André pinned Hogan and the official made a three count, even though Hogan had lifted his shoulder. It turned out that André's benefactor—Million Dollar Man, Ted DiBiase—had hired the official's twin brother and bribed him to throw the match in André's favor. Incredibly, André didn't hold on to the title—he immediately surrendered it to Million Dollar Man. This was the most-watched WWE match in history, with 33 million viewers.

**DATE OF BIRTH:** October 6, 1935
**HEIGHT:** 5ft 10in (1.78m)
**WEIGHT:** 265lbs (120kg)
**HOMETOWN:** Abruzzi, Italy / Pittsburgh, Pennsylvania
**SIGNATURE MOVE:** Bearhug—he used his powerful arms to squeeze the air out of his opponent.
**DEBUT:** Sammartino faced Dmitri Grabowski on December 17, 1959, pinning him in just 19 seconds.
**RETIRED:** Bruno teamed with Hulk Hogan to defeat King Kong Bundy and One Man Gang on August 29, 1987. He remained in WWE as a commentator until March 1988.

## IN NUMBERS ● ● ●

**4040 ›** Total number of days as WWE Champion

**187 ›** Number of sell-out Madison Square Garden events Bruno competed in

**48 ›** Seconds—the time it took to defeat Buddy Rogers for the WWE Championship

**1st ›** Two-time WWE Champion in history

Bruno Sammartino has his hand raised by the referee after defeating Buddy Rogers for the WWE Championship.

# THE LIVING LEGEND
## — BRUNO SAMMARTINO —

**HAVING GROWN UP** in Italy during World War II, Sammartino moved to the United States in 1950. After setting a world record in 1959 by bench-pressing 565lbs (256kg), Sammartino took up wrestling. He became "The Living Legend" in the ring, known for his fearlessness and unbreakable spirit.

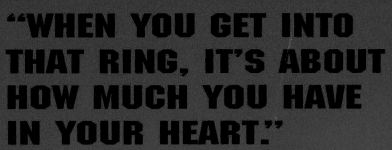

> ## "WHEN YOU GET INTO THAT RING, IT'S ABOUT HOW MUCH YOU HAVE IN YOUR HEART."
>
> BRUNO SAMMARTINO

## ★ BEST-EVER...
### ▶ SAMMARTINO RIVALS

★ **Killer Kowalski**
A bruiser known for villainous acts, Kowalski could not take Sammartino's WWE Championship in 1974 despite applying his painful hold, The Claw.

★ **Gorilla Monsoon**
This bad-tempered, 400lbs (180kg) behemoth battled Bruno many times in Madison Square Garden during the 1970s.

★ **George "The Animal" Steele**
A wildly unpredictable competitor, Steele's unsavory tactics often put Bruno down, but never for long.

★ **Ivan Koloff**
Nicknamed "The Russian Bear," Koloff shockingly ended Bruno's first title reign on January 18, 1971. Bruno later defeated Koloff in the first Steel Cage Match held at Madison Square Garden.

## 🏆 TROPHY TRIVIA

After nearly 30 years away from WWE, Bruno Sammartino was inducted into the WWE Hall of Fame on April 6, 2013. The emotional ceremony took place in his home arena, Madison Square Garden.

## IN DETAIL

### BRUNO SAMMARTINO VS. LARRY ZBYSZKO, SHOWDOWN AT SHEA (AUGUST 9, 1980)

Bruno Sammartino was heartbroken after his protégé, Larry Zbyszko, viciously attacked him. This shocking act set the stage for a Steel Cage Match at Showdown at Shea. At first, Bruno was reluctant to battle someone he still cared about, but, ever the competitor, Sammartino entered and won the brutal contest. This grudge match headlined an event that also featured Hulk Hogan against André the Giant.

## WOW! 2803

Number of days of Bruno's first reign as WWE Champion—a record that has so far proved unbeatable.

**DATE OF BIRTH:** August 11, 1953
**HEIGHT:** 6ft 8in (2.03m)
**WEIGHT:** 303lbs (137kg)
**HOMETOWN:** Venice Beach, California
**SIGNATURE MOVE:** Leg Drop—Hogan drops his leg on his opponent as they lie on the mat.
**DEBUT:** Hogan defeated Harry Valdez in November 1979, at Agricultural Hall, Pennsylvania.

## 🏆 TROPHY TRIVIA

Hulk Hogan's single reign as WWE World Tag Team Champion came on July 4, 2002, when he and Edge teamed up to defeat Billy and Chuck on *SmackDown Live*.

## IN NUMBERS ● ● ●

**8 >** Number of *WrestleMania* events headlined by Hulk Hogan

**2 >** Number of Royal Rumble Matches won by Hogan

**1st >** Superstar to host *Saturday Night Live* on March 30, 1985

**WOW!**

**6**

Number of times Hulk Hogan has held both the WWE Championship and the WCW Championship. He is the only Superstar to hold this record.

## Q: WHICH FAMOUS ACTOR INDUCTED HULK HOGAN INTO THE WWE HALL OF FAME IN 2005?

**A:** Sylvester Stallone. Hogan's co-star from *Rocky III* inducted the Hulkster into the WWE Hall of Fame on April 2, 2005.

Hulk Hogan nails longtime rival Ric Flair with his Big Boot maneuver on an episode of *RAW*. The WWE Universe knew the Hulkster's signature Leg Drop finisher would be coming next.

## ★ BEST-EVER...
### ▶ WRESTLEMANIA MATCHES

**★ WrestleMania 2 vs. King Kong Bundy**
Inside a steel cage, Hulk Hogan pinned his massive opponent to defend the WWE Title. This was the first time the Championship was ever contested at a *WrestleMania*.

**★ WrestleMania III vs. André the Giant**
In front of a record 93,173 fans, Hulk Hogan defeated André the Giant to retain his WWE Championship in March 1987.

**★ WrestleMania V vs. Randy "Macho Man" Savage**
Hulk Hogan collided with his former best friend and Mega Powers tag team partner for Savage's WWE Championship in 1989. The Hulkster won the match and began his second reign as champion.

**★ WrestleMania X8 vs. The Rock**
After being absent from WWE for almost a decade, Hulk Hogan returned to *WrestleMania X8* for a stirring Icon vs. Icon match in 2002.

## AKA

The Immortal One / "Hollywood" Hulk Hogan / The Hulkster

# THE HULKSTER
## — HULK HOGAN —

**WHEN HULK HOGAN** captured the WWE Championship from the Iron Sheik in January 1984, the era of "Hulkamania" began. For the next decade, Hulk Hogan was a dominant WWE Superstar, winning multiple WWE titles and appearing on TV programs, magazine covers, and merchandise.

**DATE OF BIRTH:** July 22, 1965
**HEIGHT:** 6ft 1in (1.85m)
**WEIGHT:** 225lbs (102kg)
**HOMETOWN:** San Antonio, Texas
**SIGNATURE MOVE:** Sweet Chin Music—a swift kick to the chin.
**DEBUT:** Michaels debuted in WWE as one half of The Rockers on June 18, 1988. He and partner Marty Jannetty were touted as "excitement personified" after defeating the Intruder and Iron Mike Sharpe.
**RETIRED:** March 28, 2010 after losing to to Undertaker at *WrestleMania XXVI*.

## AKA

HBK / The Showstopper / The Icon / Mr. *WrestleMania* / The Main Event / The Heartbreak Kid

### ROYAL RUMBLE 1995

HBK BARELY KEPT ONE FOOT OFF THE FLOOR TO STAY IN THIS MATCH, BUT HE BATTLED ON AND WON.

### WRESTLEMANIA 22

SHAWN LEAPT OFF A MASSIVE LADDER ONTO MR. MCMAHON, WHO WAS IN A TRASHCAN.

### NO MERCY 2008

A RIVALRY WITH CHRIS JERICHO REACHED A TENSE CLIMAX AS BOTH MEN REACHED FOR THE DANGLING WORLD HEAVYWEIGHT CHAMPIONSHIP AT THE SAME TIME.

## SHOWSTOPPING MOMENTS

Beyond championships and accolades, Shawn Michaels produced iconic moments in the ring which not only stole the show, but also gained him a place in history as one of WWE's most entertaining Superstars.

### RAW (APRIL 23, 2007)

SHAWN PULLED OUT ALL THE STOPS TO WIN IN A CLASH WITH JOHN CENA THAT LASTED NEARLY AN HOUR IN LONDON, ENGLAND.

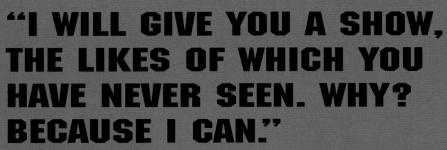

"I WILL GIVE YOU A SHOW, THE LIKES OF WHICH YOU HAVE NEVER SEEN. WHY? BECAUSE I CAN."

SHAWN MICHAELS

Shawn Michaels levels Kane with his signature move, Sweet Chin Music, on an episode of *RAW*.

# THE HEARTBREAK KID
## — SHAWN MICHAELS —

**IN A CAREER** spanning more than 25 years, Michaels delivered show-stealing performances and took pride in outperforming his peers. He shook up WWE with edgy behavior as part of the stable D-Generation X, and proved that WWE Champions can come in more compact sizes.

# THE NATURE BOY
## RIC FLAIR

**FOR ALMOST 35 YEARS**, Ric Flair was one of the most successful competitors in sports entertainment, both as an individual and as part of The Four Horseman and Evolution stables. Competing in main-event matches worldwide, Flair was known as "the stylin', profilin', limousine-riding, jet-flying, kiss-stealing, wheelin' 'n' dealin' son of a gun."

When Ric Flair placed opponents in his dreaded Figure-Four Leglock, they were often forced to submit.

## 🏆 TROPHY TRIVIA

In 2012, Ric Flair became the first Superstar to be inducted into the WWE Hall of Fame twice! He joined the institution as an individual in 2008 and then as a member of The Four Horsemen in 2012.

## EVOLUTION

As well as being a member of The Four Horsemen, Ric Flair also teamed with Triple H to form Evolution, one of the most successful stables in WWE history. All four members saw incredible success during their time in the group from 2003 to 2005.

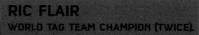

**RIC FLAIR**
WORLD TAG TEAM CHAMPION (TWICE).

**RANDY ORTON**
WORLD HEAVYWEIGHT CHAMPION AND INTERCONTINENTAL CHAMPION.

**TRIPLE H**
WORLD HEAVYWEIGHT CHAMPION (FOUR TIMES).

**BATISTA**
WORLD TAG TEAM CHAMPION (TWICE) AND *ROYAL RUMBLE* WINNER.

## INFOMANIA

**DATE OF BIRTH:** February 25, 1949
**HEIGHT:** 6ft 1in (1.85m)
**WEIGHT:** 243lbs (110kg)
**HOMETOWN:** Charlotte, North Carolina
**SIGNATURE MOVE:** Figure-Four Leglock—Flair crosses his legs with his opponent's, putting immense pressure on their knee.
**DEBUT:** Flair defeated Pete Sanchez on March 1, 1976 in Madison Square Garden.
**RETIRED:** Following his defeat by Shawn Michaels at *WrestleMania XXIV*, Flair retired from WWE on March 30, 2008.

## AKA

Slick Ric / The Dirtiest Player in the Game / The Nature Boy

# ★ BEST-EVER...

## STRATUS-FYING MATCHES

★ **Unforgiven 2002 vs. Molly Holly**
Trish overcame Holly's punishing moves in the ring to claim Women's Championship gold for the third time.

★ **Unforgiven 2006 vs. Lita**
Trish thrilled the WWE Universe by claiming the Women's Championship in an emotional battle, allowing her to retire a champion in her hometown of Toronto.

★ **WrestleMania XIX vs. Jazz vs. Victoria**
On WWE's grandest stage, Trish outlasted two of WWE's toughest female competitors in a Triple Threat Match, claiming her fourth Women's Championship.

★ **RAW (December 6, 2004) vs. Lita**
Trish became only the third woman in history to compete in a *RAW* main event.

## TITLE TRIVIA

Trish Stratus defeated Ivory, Jacqueline, Jazz, Lita, and Mighty Molly in a Six-Pack Challenge at *Survivor Series 2001* to claim her first Women's Championship.

# TRISH STRATUS

**IDOLIZED BY MANY**, Trish Stratus exploded into the WWE rings in 2000 and became one of the most iconic female Superstars. Over the next six years, she guaranteed "100% Stratusfaction" and delivered by winning seven Women's Championships—more than any other female in WWE history.

**DATE OF BIRTH:** December 18, 1975
**HEIGHT:** 5ft 5in (1.65m)
**HOMETOWN:** Toronto, Canada
**SIGNATURE MOVE:** Stratusfaction—using the top rope as a springboard, Trish floors her foe in a headlock.
**DEBUT:** In her first match, Trish won a Tag Team Match with T&A against the sibling duo Hardy Boyz and Lita on *SmackDown* on June 22, 2000.
**RETIRED:** In Trish's final match she defeated Lita at *Unforgiven* on September 17, 2006. However, she returned briefly as part of a tag team at *WrestleMania XXVII* in 2011 and on *RAW* the following night.

# "I DON'T CARE IF YOU'RE BRITNEY FREAKING SPEARS, NOBODY IS GOING TO STEAL MY SPOTLIGHT."

TRISH STRATUS

Trish Stratus awaits her opponent, Mickie James, in a Women's Championship Match at *Backlash* in April 2006.

## STRATUSFACTION

**TRISH DRIVES HER OPPONENTS FACE FIRST TO THE MAT.**

## 🏆 TROPHY TRIVIA

At *RAW's* 10th Anniversary celebration on January 14, 2003, Trish was named "Diva of the Decade," despite being in WWF for only three years.

## STRATUS-FYING MOVES

Trish defeated her opponents with a wide variety of athletic moves, allowing her to become arguably the most accomplished female Superstar in WWE history.

## CHICK KICK

**A SIMPLE YET EFFECTIVE ROUNDHOUSE KICK.**

**STRATUSPHERE**
**AN UPSIDE-DOWN TRISH LAUNCHES OPPONENTS FROM THE ROPES.**

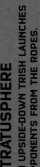

Seconds—the amount of time it took Ultimate Warrior to pin The Honky Tonk Man during the Intercontinental Championship at *SummerSlam 1988*, ending The Honky Tonk Man's 15-month reign!

## TITLE TRIVIA

Ultimate Warrior captured the WWE Championship at *WrestleMania VI*, defeating Hulk Hogan in an epic title-for-title match, that pitted Ultimate Warrior's Intercontinental Championship against Hulk Hogan's WWE title.

## Q: WHICH FUTURE WWE CHAMPION MADE HIS UNSUCCESSFUL *WRESTLEMANIA* DEBUT BY CHALLENGING ULTIMATE WARRIOR AT *WRESTLEMANIA XII*?

**A:** Triple H. While Triple H was not able to pin Ultimate Warrior at *WrestleMania XII* on March 31, 1996, he did go on to compete in nine World Title matches at *WrestleMania*.

## INFOMANIA

**DATE OF BIRTH:** June 16, 1959
**HEIGHT:** 6ft 2in (1.88m)
**WEIGHT:** 280lbs (127kg)
**HOMETOWN:** Parts unknown
**SIGNATURE MOVE:** Warrior Splash—Warrior propels himself off the ropes and slams chest-first onto his downed opponent.
**DEBUT:** Ultimate Warrior defeated Terry Gibbs on October 25, 1987.
**RETIRED:** Warrior's last major appearance was at *Halloween Havoc* on October 25, 1998.

## LEADERBOARD

Longest WWE Championship reigns of Superstars who have only held the title once.

| NAME | DAYS |
| --- | --- |
| Pedro Morales | 1,027 |
| Diesel | 358 |
| "Superstar" Billy Graham | 296 |
| Ultimate Warrior | 293 |
| JBL | 280 |

# ULTIMATE WARRIOR

**WITH HIS MANIC ENERGY**, painted face, and multicolored arm tassels, Ultimate Warrior was one of the most popular Superstars in WWE history. He famously held both the Intercontinental and WWE titles after his victory at WrestleMania VI, and was inducted into the WWE Hall of Fame in 2014.

Ultimate Warrior wears the WWE Championship to the ring weeks after defeating Hulk Hogan at *Wrestlemania VI.*

## "FEEL THE POWER OF THE ULTIMATE WARRIOR!"

ULTIMATE WARRIOR

## RESULTS TABLE

Ultimate Warrior has been more successful in *Survivor Series* elimination matches than anyone else! Over a three-year period, he faced down many opponents in four elimination matches, and was the sole survivor three times, and co-survivor once.

| | ULTIMATE WARRIOR'S TEAMMATES | OPPONENTS | WHO DID ULTIMATE WARRIOR ELIMINATE? |
|---|---|---|---|
| 1988 | Brutus Beefcake, Sam Houston, The Blue Blazer, Jim Brunzell | The Honky Tonk Man, Ron Bass, Danny Davis, Greg Valentine, Bad News Brown | Ron Bass, Greg Valentine |
| 1989 | Jim Neidhart, The Rockers (Shawn Michaels and Marty Jannetty) | The Heenan Family: Bobby Heenan, André the Giant, Haku, Arn Anderson | Arn Anderson, Bobby Heenan |
| 1990 | Texas Tornado, Legion of Doom (Hawk and Animal) | The Perfect Team: Mr. Perfect, Demolition (Ax, Smash, Crush) | Ax, Mr. Perfect |
| 1990 | Hulk Hogan, Tito Santana | Rick Martel, Warlord Hercules, Ted DiBiase, Power and Glory (Hercules and Paul Roma) | Hercules |

# AKA

"Stunning" Steve Austin / The Ringmaster / Bionic Redneck / The Texas Rattlesnake

Stone Cold victimizes Kane with his illustrious finishing move, the Stone Cold Stunner.

## IN NUMBERS ● ● ●

**529** ❯ Days as WWE Champion—more than anyone during his career

**17** ❯ Championship wins in WWE and WCW, including six WWE Championships

**8** ❯ Vehicles driven at WWE events, including a Zamboni, cement truck, monster truck, and a forklift truck

**3** ❯ Royal Rumble Match wins in 1997, 1998, and 2001—a record!

**1** ❯ *King of the Ring tournament win*

### TITLE TRIVIA

At *Backlash 2001*, reigning WWE Champion Stone Cold Steve Austin teamed up with Triple H to win the World Tag Team Championship, becoming a rare dual titleholder.

**DATE OF BIRTH:** December 18, 1964
**HEIGHT:** 6ft 2in (1.88m)
**WEIGHT:** 252lbs (114kg)
**HOMETOWN:** Victoria, Texas
**SIGNATURE MOVE:** Stone Cold Stunner — Austin grabs an opponent and drops to a seated position.
**DEBUT:** Following success in WCW and ECW, Steve Austin moved to WWE in January, 1996, under the management of Ted DiBiase. Austin was known as "The Ringmaster" for two months before becoming "Stone Cold."

# ★ BEST-EVER...

## STONE COLD CRAZY MOMENTS

★ **RAW (October 12, 1998), Cement Corvette**
Mr. McMahon could only watch as Austin filled his expensive car with cement.

★ **RAW (January 19, 1998), Boxer vs. Superstar**
Austin started a brawl on *RAW* with the fearsome boxer Mike Tyson.

★ **RAW (December 15, 1997), Intercontinental Splash**
Austin hurled The Rock's Intercontinental Championship Title off a bridge in Durham, New Hampshire into the water below.

★ **RAW (October 5, 1998), Paging Dr. Austin**
As Mr. McMahon lay in a hospital bed, Austin barged in and whacked him with a bedpan.

★ **Survivor Series (November 19, 2000), The Game Gets Played**
Using a forklift, Austin hoisted a car high off the ground and dropped it—with Triple H inside!

## 🏆 TROPHY TRIVIA

Stone Cold was inducted into the Hall of Fame in 2009 and, of course, celebrated with a beer bath in his formal attire!

> # "...AND THAT'S THE BOTTOM LINE, 'CAUSE STONE COLD SAID SO!"
> STONE COLD STEVE AUSTIN

# THE TEXAS RATTLESNAKE
# —STONE COLD STEVE AUSTIN—

**DEFIANT, BRASH**, and as mean as a rattlesnake, Stone Cold Steve Austin is everything a traditional hero is not, and the WWE Universe loves him for it. This hard-nosed competitor doesn't care who stands in his way—where he walks, a trail of wreckage follows.

When Randy Savage adopted The Macho King persona, he also employed the managerial services of Sensational Queen Sherri.

## TITLE TRIVIA

Savage won his first major WWE championship, the Intercontinental Championship, by beating Tito Santana on February 8, 1986.

## IN DETAIL

### DEBUT OF THE MEGA POWERS, *SUMMERSLAM* (AUGUST 29, 1988)

The Million Dollar Man, Ted DiBiase, enlisted the help of André the Giant in pursuit of Randy Savage's WWE Championship. But Savage had his own ally—Hulk Hogan. The two Superstars combined to form The Mega Powers tag team. They faced DiBiase and André at the first-ever *SummerSlam*, and managed to win the match with a little help from his manager, Miss Elizabeth. She distracted André and DiBiase, allowing The Mega Powers to gain the win.

## WOW!

### 59

Number of competitors Randy Savage outlasted to win the first-ever WCW World War 3 Match on November 26, 1995.

**INFOMANIA**

**DATE OF BIRTH:** November 15, 1952
**HEIGHT:** 6ft 1in (1.85m)
**WEIGHT:** 237lbs (107kg)
**HOMETOWN:** Sarasota, Florida
**SIGNATURE MOVE:** Savage Elbow Drop—an elbow drop from the top rope of the ring.
**DEBUT:** Savage defeated Aldo Marino in his WWE debut on July 6, 1985, winning the match in less than three minutes after delivering a pair of devastating top-rope elbow drops.
**RETIRED:** February 18, 2005

# THE MACHO MAN
## — RANDY SAVAGE —

**RANDY SAVAGE BROUGHT** an undeniable intensity and passion to the ring. Known for his high-risk moves, Savage was a main eventer and championship contender throughout his career. He also managed to win six World Championships, including the World Titles in both WWE and WCW.

# "THE ONLY THING THAT'S FOR SURE ABOUT STING... IS NOTHING'S FOR SURE."

STING

Sting wows the crowds as he arrives for his match against Triple H at *WrestleMania 31* wearing a glitzy red coat.

## STARS AND STRIPES

STING WAS DECKED OUT IN A PATRIOTIC OUTFIT FOR *THE GREAT AMERICAN BASH 1990*.

## GREEN GET-UP

STING SHOWED OFF A SEQUIN GREEN AND GOLD JACKET AT *STARRCADE 1990*.

## BIG MATCH OUTFITS

Sting was known to vary the colors and designs of his iconic appearance. For matches with special significance, he unveiled flashy new outfits crafted just for the occasion.

## GLITTERING GOLD

STING WORE A PURPLE AND GOLD JACKET DURING HIS SURFER ERA IN THE EARLY 1990S.

## BLINDING BLUE

IN THE MID-1990S, ORANGE TASSELS WITH METALLIC BLUE MADE AN IMPACT.

## AKA

The Franchise of WCW / The Vigilante / The Icon

### INFOMANIA

**DATE OF BIRTH:** March 20, 1959
**HEIGHT:** 6ft 2in (1.88m)
**WEIGHT:** 250lbs (113kg)
**HOMETOWN:** Venice Beach, California
**SIGNATURE MOVE:** Scorpion Death Drop—Sting sweeps his trapped opponent backward and down.
**DEBUT:** Sting first competed in 1985 under the name Flash Borden. His tag team partner was the man who would become Ultimate Warrior in WWE.
**RETIRED:** Sting announced his retirement during his WWE Hall of Fame induction speech on April 2, 2016.

### TELL ME MORE

In 1996, a nWo imposter tricked everyone into believing Sting had joined the malicious group. Sting felt betrayed by WCW for doubting his loyalty. As a result, he became a silent, brooding personality—abandoning his neon look in favor of a more gothic, black and white appearance.

### ★ BEST-EVER...

#### "NOTHING'S FOR SURE" MOMENTS

★ *Survivor Series 2014,* **Surprise Sting**
After nearly 30 years in sports entertainment, Sting finally appeared in WWE. He dropped in unannounced during the main event and attacked WWE COO, Triple H.

★ *Uncensored 1997,* **Bat Attack**
With fans fearing that Sting might join the nWo, he put everyone at ease by attacking the villainous faction with his signature baseball bat.

★ *Nitro (June 1, 1998),* **Red Allegiance**
Sting delighted fans by siding with the nWo Wolfpac splinter faction. He then changed his signature face paint to red to show his new allegiance.

# THE ICON
## — STING —

**STING SET THE** sports entertainment scene ablaze with his neon face paint, high-pitched war cry, and vibrant personality. Originally part of the WCW brand in the 1990s, Sting joined WWE in 2014. He announced his retirement in 2016, after more than 30 years in the business.

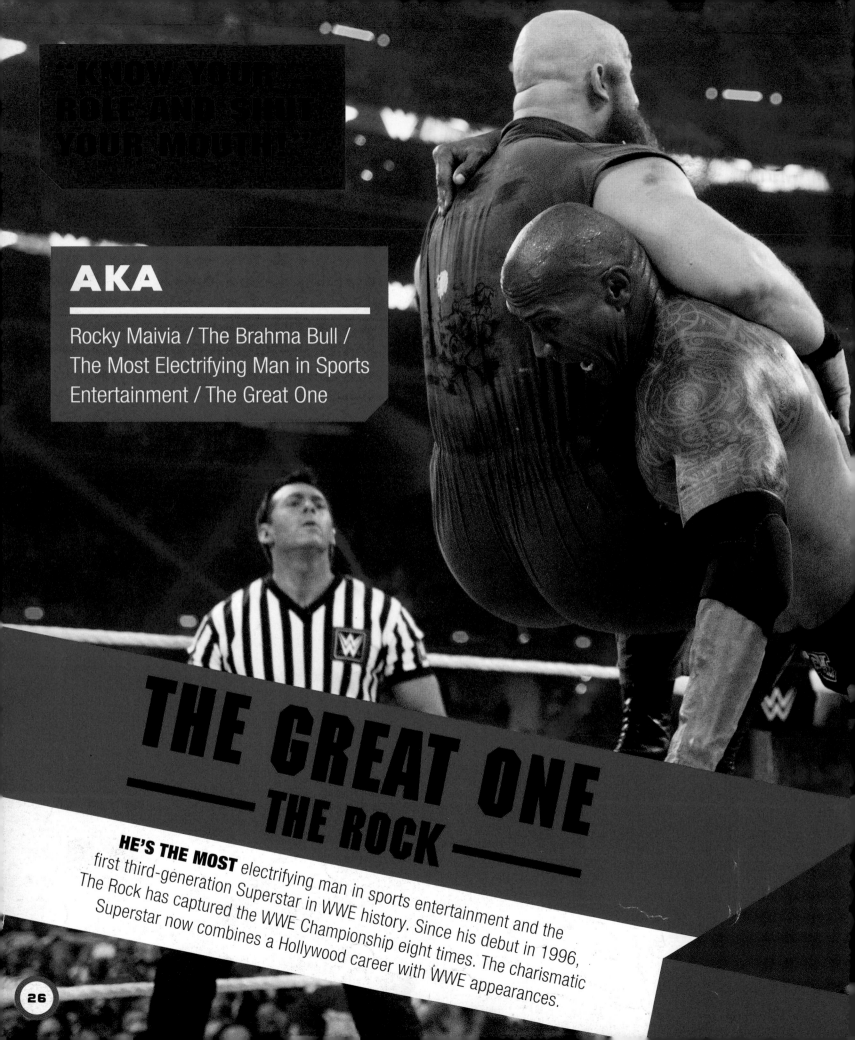

"KNOW YOUR ROLE AND SHUT YOUR MOUTH!"

## AKA

Rocky Maivia / The Brahma Bull / The Most Electrifying Man in Sports Entertainment / The Great One

# THE GREAT ONE
## THE ROCK

**HE'S THE MOST** electrifying man in sports entertainment and the first third-generation Superstar in WWE history. Since his debut in 1996, The Rock has captured the WWE Championship eight times. The charismatic Superstar now combines a Hollywood career with WWE appearances.

## INFOMANIA

**DATE OF BIRTH:** May 2, 1972
**HEIGHT:** 6ft 5in (1.96m)
**WEIGHT:** 260lbs (118kg)
**HOMETOWN:** Miami, Florida
**SIGNATURE MOVE:** People's Elbow—The Rock gains momentum by rebounding off the ropes and drops his elbow onto the chest of his foe as they lie flat on the mat.
**DEBUT:** The Rock was the sole survivor in the *Survivor Series* Match on November 17, 1996 in Madison Square Garden.

## TITLE TRIVIA

The Rock ends his match with Erick Rowan with a high-powered Rock Bottom maneuver at *WrestleMania 32*.

### WRESTLEMANIA XV
STONE COLD ENDED THE ROCK'S WWE CHAMPIONSHIP REIGN, DESPITE THE ROCK HAVING THE CORPORATION ON HIS SIDE.

### WRESTLEMANIA X-7
ONCE AGAIN, STONE COLD CAPTURED THE WWE TITLE FROM THE ROCK, BUT TOOK HELP FROM MR. MCMAHON TO DO SO.

### WRESTLEMANIA XIX
THE ROCK FINALLY DEFEATED STONE COLD IN WHAT BECAME AUSTIN'S LAST WWE MATCH.

## THE ROCK VS. STONE COLD

They were the first Superstars to compete against each other in three *WrestleMania* events. Twice, Stone Cold Steve Austin and The Rock battled for the WWE Championship. They then met one last time in Austin's final wrestling match on March 30, 2003.

# "THE BEST THERE IS, THE BEST THERE WAS, THE BEST THERE EVER WILL BE."

BRET HART

## Q: IN WHAT YEARS DID BRET HART WIN THE *KING OF THE RING* TOURNAMENT?

**A:** 1991 and 1993. Since no tournament took place in 1992, his second victory made him a back-to-back winner. Nearly 25 years later, he is still the only Superstar to win the coveted crown twice.

## ★ BEST-EVER...

### HART-POUNDING MATCHES

★ *Coliseum Home Video* (July 1992) vs. Shawn Michaels
Hart competed in and won the first Ladder Match in WWE history, defending his Intercontinental Championship against his rival.

★ *SummerSlam* (August 29, 1992) vs. British Bulldog
Hart contended with his brother-in-law and a partisan London audience. He lost his Intercontinental Title to the Superstar, but earned the crowd's respect for his valiant performance.

★ *WrestleMania XIII* vs. Roddy Piper
In a classic back-and-forth struggle, the "Hit Man" finally triumphed, and claimed his second Intercontinental Championship, in April 1992.

★ *SummerSlam* (August 29, 1994) vs. Owen Hart
For several months, Hart's younger brother pursued his WWE Title. Bret finally proved his superiority in a dangerous Steel Cage Match.

Bret Hart locks the mighty Undertaker in his Sharpshooter move, proving that no one is safe from his celebrated submission hold.

## INFOMANIA

**DATE OF BIRTH:** July 2, 1957

**HEIGHT:** 6ft (1.82m)

**WEIGHT:** 235lbs (106kg)

**HOMETOWN:** Calgary, Canada

**SIGNATURE MOVE:** Sharpshooter—Hart traps a Superstar face down and wrenches both legs backward.

**DEBUT:** Hart first competed in Calgary before debuting in a WWE match on August 29, 1984. On his arrival, he promised to make the fans proud of him. However, he went on to gain notoriety as a villain and a member of hostile faction The Hart Foundation.

**RETIRED:** October 27, 2000

## WOW! 17

Total number of Championship wins in WWE and WCW, including World, Intercontinental, United States, and Tag Team Titles.

# THE EXCELLENCE OF EXECUTION
## BRET "HIT MAN" HART

**TRAINED BY** his father in a basement dubbed "The Dungeon," Bret Hart became the Superstar who set the bar for pure wrestling acumen. A no-nonsense competitor, Hart dazzled spectators with his ability to expose weaknesses in the ring and used his skills to capture every major title in WWE.

# LEADERBOARD

The longest-reigning American Wrestling Association (AWA) and National Wrestling Alliance (NWA) champions, active before the start of WWE, inducted into the WWE Hall of Fame.

| PROMOTION | SUPERSTAR | TOTAL TIME AS CHAMPION | INDUCTED |
|---|---|---|---|
| | | | |

Up to the end of 2017, 154 Superstars, celebrities, and people who have shown courage in their personal life have been honored in the WWE Hall of Fame.

Former Olympic gold medalist Kurt Angle held the WWE Championship four times before being inducted into the WWE Hall of Fame in 2017.

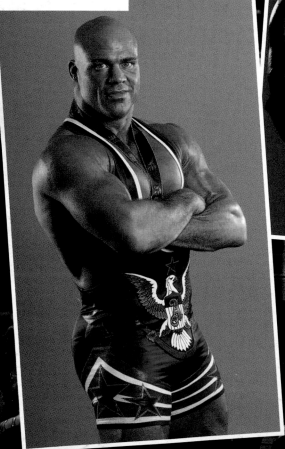

After holding 10 different championships in WCW, Diamond Dallas Page entered the WWE Hall of Fame in 2017.

## Q: WHO GAVE THE INDUCTION SPEECH FOR 2013 CELEBRITY INDUCTEE AND FUTURE PRESIDENT OF THE UNITED STATES, DONALD TRUMP?

**A:** Mr. McMahon. The WWE Chairman and CEO inducted his rival from *WrestleMania 23*'s *Battle of the Billionaires*.

2006
BRET "HIT MAN" HART.

## THE GREATS RETURN

No matter how long an absence from sports entertainment, several Superstars have made emotional returns to WWE for their induction into the Hall of Fame.

2010
WENDI RICHTER.

2013
BRUNO SAMMARTINO.

2014
ULTIMATE WARRIOR.

## WOW!

**11**

Out of the first 13 men to hold the WWE Championship are members of the WWE Hall of Fame.

## 🏆 TROPHY TRIVIA

The First WWE Champion in history, Buddy Rogers, was added to the WWE Hall of Fame in 1994.

# WWE HALL OF FAME

**FOR ANYONE INVOLVED** in professional wrestling, there is no greater way to cap off your career than to be inducted into the WWE Hall of Fame. The annual ceremony is where Superstars of the past, present, and future gather together to honor the rich history of WWE.

Undertaker and Brock Lesnar exchange hard-hitting blows prior to their showdown at *WrestleMania 30*.

# SUPERSTARS OF TODAY

02

**DATE OF BIRTH:** April 23, 1977
**HEIGHT:** 6ft 1in (1.85m)
**WEIGHT:** 251lbs (114kg)
**HOMETOWN:** West Newbury, Massachusetts
**SIGNATURE MOVE:** Attitude Adjustment——Cena hoists his opponent into a fireman's lift and slams them down onto the mat.
**DEBUT:** Cena answered an open challenge to battle the Superstar Kurt Angle on the June 27, 2002 episode of *SmackDown*. Cena was so impressive, Undertaker personally congratulated him backstage.

## WOW!

# 1412

Combined length of Cena's 16 World Championship reigns in days.

## AKA

The Doctor of Thuganomics / The Chain Gang Leader / The Cenation Leader / The Face That Runs The Place / The Champ

## IN NUMBERS ● ● ● ●

**89** ❯ Wins in pay-per-view matches

**25** ❯ Championship wins

**5-0** ❯ Record in "I Quit" Matches

**5** ❯ Number of times Cena has headlined *WrestleMania*

# THE CHAMP
## — JOHN CENA —

**TO JOHN CENA,** "hustle, loyalty, respect" is not a slogan. It is the code by which he lives, in and out of the ring. Cena's unrivalled work ethic has made him the cornerstone of WWE for more than a decade and has led him to become one of the most successful Superstars in the WWE ring.

John Cena holds The Rock in his powerful finisher, the Attitude Adjustment.

## ★ BEST-EVER...

### ▶ CENA CHAMPIONSHIP PERFORMANCES

**★ WrestleMania 21 vs. JBL**
Cena brought the self-proclaimed "Wrestling God" and reigning WWE Champion JBL down from his perch. After JBL's signature Clothesline From Hell finishing move missed its mark, Cena flattened him with an Attitude Adjustment. Seconds later, Cena hoisted his first WWE Championship over his head in triumph.

**★ Bragging Rights 2009 vs. Randy Orton**
The Champ put his employment as a *RAW* Superstar on the line in a 60-minute Iron Man Match. Cena persevered and forced his archrival, Randy Orton, to submit, claiming the WWE Championship.

**★ Unforgiven 2006 vs. Edge**
In Edge's home city of Toronto, Canada, Cena bested Edge in a Tables, Ladders, and Chairs Match. Cena hurled his villainous foe from a ladder and sent him crashing through two stacked tables!

## "NEVER GIVE UP."
JOHN CENA

## IN DETAIL

## JOHN CENA VS. THE ROCK, *WRESTLEMANIA 29* (APRIL 7, 2013)

In this historic WWE Championship rematch, both competitors were cautious early in the match, not wanting to make a devastating mistake. Later, both competitors emptied their offensive arsenals, but neither would succumb to the other's attempts at victory. Finally, Cena's Attitude Adjustment move sent The Rock flailing into the mat below. The referee pounded the canvas three times, ending both the match and John Cena's long-standing rivalry with The Rock.

Randy Orton can hit anyone with his signature RKO at any time, as The Miz found out on *SmackDown Live* in July 2016.

### TITLE TRIVIA

Randy Orton won his first championship, the Intercontinental Championship, by defeating Rob Van Dam on December 14, 2003.

# THE VIPER
## —RANDY ORTON—

**A THIRD-GENERATION SUPERSTAR**, Randy Orton has been a dangerous competitor in WWE for more than 15 years. His speed, skill, and dominant performances in the ring have helped to make him one of the most successful Superstars of all time.

**DATE OF BIRTH:** April 1, 1980
**HEIGHT:** 6ft 5in (1.96m)
**WEIGHT:** 235lbs (106kg)
**HOMETOWN:** St. Louis, Missouri
**SIGNATURE MOVE:** RKO—Orton wraps his arms around a Superstar and drops them to the mat.
**DEBUT:** Defeated Hardcore Holly on *SmackDown Live* on April 25, 2002 at Peoria Civic Center, Illinois.

## IN NUMBERS ● ● ●

**48:27 ❯** Time Orton spent in the ring at the 2009 *Royal Rumble*. He entered ninth and won the match

**15 ❯** Length in minutes of Randy Orton's first WWE title reign. Mr. McMahon awarded Orton the title at the start of *No Mercy 2007*, but Triple H defeated him in the show's opening match

**8 ❯** Seconds—the time it took to defeat Daniel Bryan for the WWE Championship at *SummerSlam 2013*, when Orton cashed in his *Money in the Bank* opportunity

## WOW! 24

The age at which Orton won the World Heavyweight Championship in 2004, is one of the youngest champion in the history of the title.

## STABLE SUCCESS

Randy Orton has been a member of some of the most ruthless and powerful stables in WWE history.

### EVOLUTION
WITH RIC FLAIR, TRIPLE H, AND BATISTA.

### LEGACY
WITH CODY RHODES AND TED DIBIASE.

### THE WYATT FAMILY
WITH LUKE HARPER AND BRAY WYATT.

### THE AUTHORITY
WITH SETH ROLLINS, KANE, TRIPLE H, AND STEPHANIE MCMAHON.

## DEADLIEST MATCHES

During his reign of terror, Undertaker has helped introduce several dangerous match types. These matches have created hair-raising bouts with The Deadman's unfortunate foes.

### INFERNO MATCH
UNDERTAKER SET HIS OWN BROTHER, THE SUPERSTAR KANE, ON FIRE!

### CASKET MATCH
HEIDENREICH IS ENTOMBED IN A CASKET BY UNDERTAKER.

### LAST RIDE MATCH
UNDERTAKER SENT MR. KENNEDY FOR A RIDE IN A HEARSE.

### HELL IN A CELL
RANDY ORTON STEPPED INTO HELL WITH THE DEADMAN AND PAID THE PRICE.

The ominous toll of a bell, chilling darkness, and plenty of smoke and fire are all part of Undertaker's spine-tingling entrance to the ring.

## WOW! 23

Wins at *WrestleMania*—equal to the combined number of wins for John Cena, The Rock, and Hulk Hogan!

# THE DEADMAN
## — UNDERTAKER —

**UNDERTAKER HAS CAST** a menacing shadow over WWE since 1990. He has created a virtual graveyard, with the names of many legendary Superstars adorning the headstones. No one in WWE history has been more feared, respected, and accomplished than The Deadman.

## "REST IN PEACE!"

UNDERTAKER

# ★ BEST-EVER...

## DEADMAN MOMENTS

★ *Funeral Parlor (February 29, 1992), Cheers not Jeers*
Unpopular Superstar Jake "The Snake" Roberts appeared on Paul Bearer's grim talk show and asked Undertaker whose side he was on. Fans cheered Undertaker for the first time when he replied, "Not yours!"

★ *SummerSlam 1994, Dark Doppelgänger*
After a doppelgänger of Undertaker was introduced in the summer of 1994, the real Undertaker emerged at *SummerSlam* and defeated the imposter by hitting him with his Tombstone move—three times!

★ *RAW (April 26, 1999), Forced Marriage*
Undertaker attempted to force Stephanie McMahon to marry him with help from his evil minions in the Ministry of Darkness stable.

★ *Royal Rumble 2007, Rumble Winner*
Entering the match in the final 30th spot, Undertaker outlasted all the other competitors and eliminated Shawn Michaels last to win his first Royal Rumble Match in his 17th year in WWE.

## THROUGH THE AGES

**Original Deadman:** The mysterious Undertaker rarely spoke and seemingly derived power from a mystical urn.
**Ministry Leader:** A more demonic-looking Undertaker formed a sinister stable called the Ministry of Darkness.
**Big Evil:** Showing a more human side, Undertaker rode a Harley to the ring and began wearing leather vests and blue jeans.
**Deadman Resurrected:** After Kane buried him alive, Undertaker returned as his former self. Since then he has ruled WWE with a vengeance!

## INFOMANIA

**BORN:** March 24, 1965
**HEIGHT:** 6ft 10in (2.08m)
**WEIGHT:** 309lbs (140kg)
**HOMETOWN:** Death Valley, California
**SIGNATURE MOVES:** Tombstone—Undertaker lowers an upside-down opponent forcefully to the mat. Last Ride—an opponent is thrust high in the air before being slammed onto his back.
**DEBUT:** Undertaker was revealed as the mystery fourth member of The Million Dollar Man Ted DiBiase's team at *Survivor Series 1990*. Seemingly raised from a graveyard, his deathly appearance frightened spectators. The equally ghoulish Paul Bearer soon became his manager.

**DATE OF BIRTH:** July 12, 1977
**HEIGHT:** 6ft 3in (1.90m)
**WEIGHT:** 286lb (130kg)
**HOMETOWN:** Minneapolis, Minnesota
**SIGNATURE MOVE:** The F5—Lesnar drapes his opponent across his shoulders and spins him.
**DEBUT:** Lesnar defeated Jeff Hardy at *Backlash 2002* on April 21, 2002.

## AKA

The Next Big Thing /
The 1 in 21-1 /
The Beast Incarnate

## 🏆 TROPHY TRIVIA

In addition to being a multi-time WWE Champion, Brock Lesnar has won Heavyweight titles in the NCAA in wrestling and the UFC in mixed martial arts.

## ★ BEST-EVER...

### SUMMERSLAM MATCHES

★ *SummerSlam 2012* **vs. Triple H**
Earlier in 2012, Lesnar broke Triple H's arm when he refused to re-negotiate Lesnar's contract. Triple H sought his revenge at *SummerSlam*, but Lesnar forced him to submit to his Kimura Lock move in a No Disqualification Match.

★ *SummerSlam 2013* **vs. CM Punk**
CM Punk's manager, Paul Heyman, betrayed Punk and had his other client, Brock Lesnar, attack Punk. Punk and Lesnar then engaged in an epic slugfest at *SummerSlam* where Lesnar pinned Punk after delivering a powerful F5 move on his opponent, slamming him onto a chair.

★ *SummerSlam 2014* **vs. John Cena**
Brock Lesnar captured the WWE Championship from John Cena by subjecting Cena to an astounding 16 suplexes during the match.

★ *SummerSlam 2016* **vs. Randy Orton**
After an absence from WWE, Lesnar returned to battle with Randy Orton. The match was so brutal the referee decided to stop proceedings and award Lesnar a TKO (Technical Knock Out).

# THE BEAST INCARNATE
## BROCK LESNAR

**HE IS A FORCE** of destruction who swept through WWE from 2002, only to depart in 2004 to conquer the UFC. After becoming the UFC Heavyweight Champion, Brock Lesnar shocked the WWE Universe by returning in spectacular fashion, ending Undertaker's winning streak and re-capturing the WWE Championship.

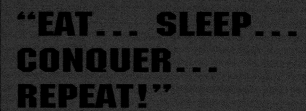

Brock Lesnar delivers an F5 to Randy Orton on his way to a dominant victory at *SummerSlam 2016*.

### FIRST ROUND MATCH
DEFEATED BUBBA RAY DUDLEY.

### QUARTERFINALS
PINNED BOOKER T.

### SEMIFINALS
PINNED TEST.

### FINALS
PINNED ROB VAN DAM.

## KING OF THE RING

Lesner defeated four opponents to win the 2002 *King of the Ring* tournament and his first World Title opportunity—a shot at The Rock's WWE Undisputed Championship at *SummerSlam 2002*.

**DATE OF BIRTH:** June 2, 1977
**HEIGHT:** 5ft 11in (1.80m)
**WEIGHT:** 218lbs (99kg)
**HOMETOWN:** Gainesville, Georgia
**SIGNATURE MOVE:** Styles Clash—AJ Styles hoists a Superstar up by their legs and drops them face-down on the mat.
**DEBUT:** AJ Styles was a surprise entrant in the 2016 Royal Rumble Match. As the third Superstar to enter the 30-man match, AJ quickly tossed out Tyler Breeze and Curtis Axel, lasting 28 minutes before being eliminated.

AJ Styles takes aim at The Miz with his powerful Phenomenal Forearm move.

## IN DETAIL

### DEAN AMBROSE VS. AJ STYLES, *BACKLASH 2016* (SEPTEMBER 11, 2016)

Styles' victory at *SummerSlam* 2016 earned him this WWE Championship opportunity. Styles was confident at the outset, but Ambrose was equal to his offense. Styles was launched over the barricade but recovered and avoided Ambrose's Dirty Deeds finishing move. Seeing the referee unfocused, Styles hit his opponent below the belt to set up his own finisher: the Styles Clash. AJ pinned Ambrose for the Title and showed no remorse for his underhand tactics.

### 🏆 TROPHY TRIVIA

WWE Magazine named Styles "Superstar of the Year" for 2016 in its annual Best of WWE special.

# THE PHENOMENAL ONE
## — AJ STYLES —

**HE MAY BE ARROGANT,** but since his recent arrival in WWE, AJ Styles has proven he is what he has always claimed to be in the ring—phenomenal. With a WWE Championship already on his resume, there is no predicting just how dominant Styles might become.

**A:** Chris Jericho. After earning mutual respect in competitions against each other, Styles and Jericho later formed a team called Y2AJ. Together, they defeated The New Day and The Social Outcasts. Despite their success, Jericho eventually became jealous of the attention Styles was getting and turned on his partner.

## ★ BEST-EVER...

### PHENOMENAL VICTORIES

★ *No Mercy 2016* vs. Dean Ambrose vs. John Cena
AJ's first WWE Championship reign got off to an impressive start. Despite being caught in both opponents' submission moves, Styles eventually pinned John Cena to retain his title.

★ *TLC 2016* vs. Dean Ambrose
Defending the WWE Championship, Styles pulled out all the stops. He put Dean Ambrose through a table with a 450 Splash flipping maneuver on his way to victory.

★ *SummerSlam 2016* vs. John Cena
Unlike Styles' first victory over the legendary Superstar John Cena, AJ needed no assistance from his allies in The Club, and left no doubt he and Cena were on the same level. Soon after, Styles declared himself the new "Face that Runs the Place," stealing Cena's moniker.

## "EVEN ON YOUR BEST DAY, YOU CAN'T BEAT ME."

AJ STYLES

**TITLE TRIVIA**

Triple H earned his first title
on October 21, 1996 for the
Intercontinental Championship—
his first title in WWE.

## AKA

Triple H / Hunter Hearst Helmsley / The Cerebral Assassin / The King of Kings / The Game

## INFOMANIA

**DATE OF BIRTH:** July 27, 1969
**HEIGHT:** 6ft 4in (1.93m)
**WEIGHT:** 255lbs (116kg)
**HOMETOWN:** Greenwich, Connecticut
**SIGNATURE MOVE:** Pedigree—Triple H locks his opponent's arms behind him and slams him chest-first to the floor.
**DEBUT:** Triple H, who performed under the name Hunter Hearst Helmsley at the time, debuted on *Wrestling Challenge* on April 30, 1995.

## IN NUMBERS ● ● ●

**33** ❯ Competitors eliminated by Triple H from Royal Rumble Matches

**14** ❯ Total number of world championships won

**14** ❯ Years between first and second *Royal Rumble* victories—a record span

**7** ❯ Closing matches of *WrestleMania* events

## Q: TRIPLE H PLAYED A VILLAINOUS CHARACTER NAMED JARKO GRIMWOOD IN WHAT MOVIE BASED ON A MARVEL CHARACTER?

**A:** *Blade: Trinity.*

Triple H drops Roman Reigns to the mat with a Pedigree in the main event of *Wrestlemania 32*.

# THE GAME
## — TRIPLE H —

**TRIPLE H** has been a key contender at WWE main events for decades and has won more than a dozen world championships. Although he now spends most of his time in the boardroom as the Chief Operating Officer of WWE, he still competes, making an appearance as recently as *WrestleMania 33*.

## ENTER THE GAME

Throughout his career, Triple H has had some of the more inventive and entertaining *WrestleMania* entrances.

### WRESTLEMANIA 22
DRESSED AS A BARBARIAN KING.

### WRESTLEMANIA 21
LIVE PERFORMANCE BY METAL BAND, MOTÖRHEAD.

### WRESTLEMANIA XXVII
ACCOMPANIED BY A CADRE OF WARRIORS.

**WOW!**

# 4

Number of *Elimination Chamber* matches Triple H has won—more than any other Superstar in WWE history.

### WRESTLEMANIA 31
TERMINATOR-INSPIRED ENTRANCE.

> "I AM THE GAME, AND I'M THAT DAMN GOOD."
>
> TRIPLE H

## INFOMANIA

**NAMES:** Mr. McMahon, Stephanie McMahon, Shane McMahon
**HOMETOWN:** Greenwich, Connecticut
**DEBUTS:** Mr. McMahon was first seen on screen as an announcer in the 1970s. Shane began his WWE career as a referee in the late 1980s and Stephanie debuted in April 1999 when she was abducted by Undertaker!

# THE MCMAHON FAMILY

**IN WWE**, nothing happens unless the McMahon family allows it and the buck stops with Mr. McMahon, a respected and almighty tycoon. Daughter Stephanie began working in WWE as a teenager, modeling Superstar merchandise, while son Shane got his WWE start as a referee.

# "YOU'RE FIRED!"
MR. MCMAHON

## ★ BEST-EVER...
### FAMILY FEUDS

★ **No Mercy 2003, Mr. McMahon vs. Stephanie McMahon**
Unsatisfied with Stephanie's performance as *SmackDown* General Manager, Mr. McMahon arranged an "I Quit" Match against his daughter and won. Stephanie lost her position.

★ **Invasion 2001, WWE vs. The Alliance**
Shane and Stephanie joined forces to align WCW and ECW Superstars in an attempt to take down their father's company, WWE.

★ **WrestleMania X-7, Mr. McMahon vs. Shane McMahon**
Shane landed a Coast-to-Coast move on his father during a Street Fight Match. He flew across the ring and drove a trashcan into his dad to secure the win.

★ **Armageddon 1999, Mr. McMahon vs. Triple H**
Stephanie helped Triple H defeat Mr. McMahon, revealing her true feelings for her father's enemy.

## TITLE TRIVIA

Despite not being everyday competitors, each of the three McMahons has captured a championship. Shane has been European and Hardcore Champion. Stephanie held the Women's Championship, and Mr. McMahon has been WWE and ECW Champion.

## WOW! 35
The number of years that Mr. McMahon has been WWE Chairman and CEO.

## IN DETAIL

### STEPHANIE MCMAHON VS. SHANE MCMAHON, *RAW* (JULY 11, 2016)

Shane McMahon had not been seen in WWE for nearly seven years. Meanwhile, Stephanie remained with her father's company, holding several executive roles. In February 2016, Shane McMahon returned to WWE to seize authority from his sister, Stephanie. Shane tried and failed to get his desired job by winning a Hell in a Cell Match against Undertaker at *WrestleMania 32*, but he showed incredible tenacity. After months of seeing his children's leadership skills on display, Mr. McMahon awarded them separate rosters on *RAW* and *SmackDown* to oversee. The McMahon siblings have since competed tooth-and-nail to prove who possesses the superior brand.

# GENERAL MANAGERS

**BOTH *SMACKDOWN* AND *RAW*** need experienced guiding hands to run the brands' day-to-day operations as General Managers. Who better to do it than two former world champions? Daniel Bryan got his first management job on *SmackDown*. Mick Foley took the reins on *RAW* before Kurt Angle replaced him.

## INFOMANIA

**NAME:** Daniel Bryan
**DATE OF BIRTH:** May 22, 1981
**HEIGHT:** 5ft 10in (1.78m)
**WEIGHT:** 210lbs (95kg)
**HOMETOWN:** Aberdeen, Washington
**DEBUT:** Daniel Bryan lost to Chris Jericho in his first WWE match on the debut episode of *NXT* on February 23, 2010. On July 18, 2016, Daniel Bryan was introduced as *SmackDown Live* General Manager by Shane McMahon who hoped Bryan could use his experience to guide other Superstars.

**"YES! YES! YES!"**
DANIEL BRYAN

As General Manager of *SmackDown Live*, Daniel Bryan has been able to give several up-and-coming Superstars championship opportunities.

## AKA

The Beard / The "Yes" Man

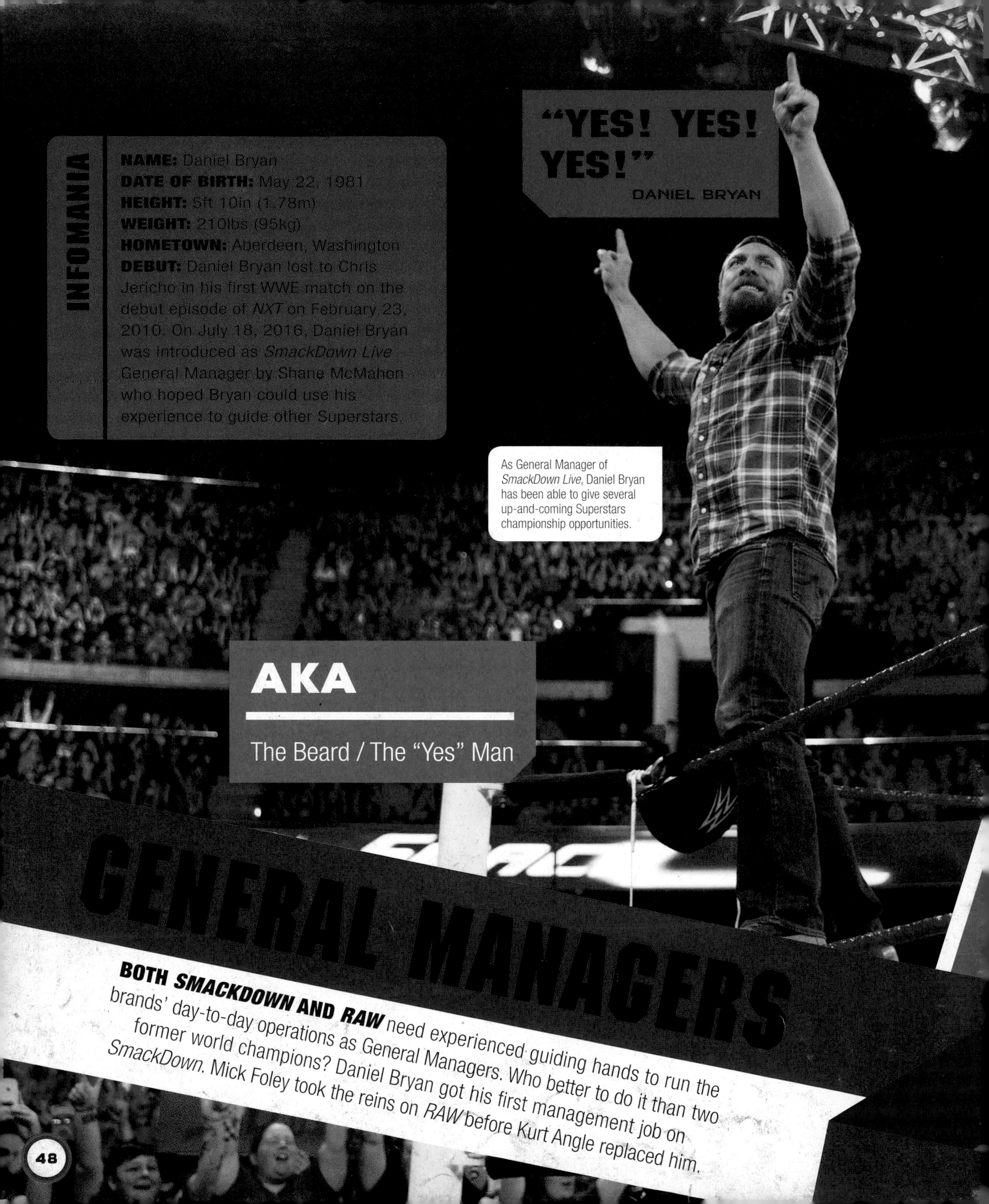

**INFOMANIA**

NAME: Mick Foley
DATE OF BIRTH:
HEIGHT:
WEIGHT: 287 lbs (130 kg)
HOMETOWN:
DEBUT:
on *RAW* on April
ever WWE match. Mick Foley
ran *RAW* in June 2000 but he
fired by Mr. McMahon in December
that year. Stephanie McMahon
reinstated him as General Manager
on July 18, 2016.

## AKA

Cactus Jack / Mankind / Dude Love / The Hardcore Legend

Before Mick Foley became General Manager of *RAW*, he had been in charge of the brand as Commissioner on three occasions since 2000.

## TELL ME MORE

*RAW* and *SmackDown* are not the only WWE brands to have General Managers. William Regal has overseen NXT since 2014. During his tenure, NXT has expanded from its Florida base to touring the globe and has added the Dusty Rhodes Tag Team Classic tournament to its events.

## "HAVE A NICE DAY!"

MICK FOLEY

49

# 220

The number of days Seth Rollins held the WWE Championship in 2015.

Seth Rollins unleashes a brutal Pedigree move on his former Shield teammate, Dean Ambrose.

## INFOMANIA

**DATE OF BIRTH:** May 28, 1986
**HEIGHT:** 6ft 1in (1.85m)
**WEIGHT:** 217lbs (98kg)
**HOMETOWN:** Davenport, Iowa
**SIGNATURE MOVE:** Pedigree—a move made famous by Triple H. Rollins locks his opponent's arms behind him and slams him chest-first to the floor.
**DEBUT:** Seth Rollins debuted at *Survivor Series 2012* as part of the defiant trio known as The Shield. Prior to that, Seth achieved notable success in NXT, becoming the brand's first champion.

## "I AM THE LIVING, BREATHING EMBODIMENT OF THE FUTURE."

SETH ROLLINS

## POLL RESULT

Prior to the June 2016 WWE Draft, wwe.com asked, "Who would you select as the number one overall pick?" Days later, RAW followed the WWE Universe and took Rollins with the first pick.

| 20% | 18% | 15% | 13% |
|-----|-----|-----|-----|
| Seth Rollins | John Cena | Brock Lesnar | AJ Styles |

## TITLE TRIVIA

At *SummerSlam 2015*, WWE World Champion Seth Rollins defeated United States Champion John Cena and became the first Superstar to hold both prestigious titles simultaneously.

## ROLLINS RISES

On Seth Rollins' path to greatness in WWE, he became notorious for both thrilling and shocking wins.

### PAYBACK 2014

SETH AND THE SHIELD PROVE THEIR DOMINANCE IN A WIN OVER EVOLUTION.

### MONEY IN THE BANK 2014

AFTER JOINING THE AUTHORITY, ROLLINS CLAIMS THE *MONEY IN THE BANK* BRIEFCASE.

### WRESTLEMANIA 31

ROLLINS SHOCKS ALL BY WINNING THE WWE CHAMPIONSHIP.

### MONEY IN THE BANK 2016

ROLLINS WINS HIS SECOND WORLD TITLE AGAINST FORMER TEAMMATE ROMAN REIGNS.

### 🏆 TROPHY TRIVIA

Weeks after injuring his knee, Rollins accepted the Slammy Award for the 2015 Superstar of the Year. He vowed to "redesign, rebuild, and reclaim" his place at the top of WWE.

# SETH ROLLINS

**THERE IS NOTHING** Seth Rollins can't do inside a WWE ring—only things he hasn't done yet! A versatile athlete, Seth is capable of slugging it out with the biggest bruisers and flying through the air like a cruiserweight. It is no exaggeration when he calls himself "The Man."

# LEADERBOARD

Longest United States Championship reigns during the WWE era of the title (2003—present).

| SUPERSTAR | LENGTH OF REIGN |
| --- | --- |
| Dean Ambrose | 351 days |
| MVP | 343 days |
| Shelton Benjamin | 240 days |
| Cesaro | 239 days |
| The Miz | 224 days |
| Chris Benoit | 222 days |
| Dolph Ziggler | 182 days |
| Sheamus | 182 days |
| Daniel Bryan | 176 days |
| Orlando Jordan | 173 days |

## WOW! 1

Dean Ambrose was *SmackDown*'s first pick in the 2016 WWE Draft, bringing with him the WWE Championship.

## TITLE TRIVIA

On December 13, 2015, Dean Ambrose beat Kevin Owens to win the Intercontinental Championship for the first time in his career.

## "MY MIND IS A VERY DANGEROUS PLACE TO BE."

DEAN AMBROSE

Dean Ambrose and AJ Styles each gave their all in their bitter rivalry for the WWE Championship on *SmackDown Live* in September 2016.

## INFOMANIA

**DATE OF BIRTH:** December 7, 1985
**HEIGHT:** 6ft 4in (1.93m)
**WEIGHT:** 225lbs (102kg)
**HOMETOWN:** Cincinnati, Ohio
**SIGNATURE MOVE:** Dirty Deeds—a headlock into a forward sweep of the legs.
**DEBUT:** Ambrose teamed with Seth Rollins and Roman Reigns to defeat Ryback and Team Hell No in a Tables, Ladders, and Chairs Match on November 18, 2012.

## Q: WHAT IS THE NAME OF THE *RAW* INTERVIEW SEGMENT HOSTED BY DEAN AMBROSE?

**A:** *Ambrose Asylum*. Ambrose welcomes fellow WWE Superstars to be grilled by him on the show.

## IN DETAIL

### MONEY IN THE BANK (JUNE 19, 2016)

In perhaps the greatest night of his WWE career, Dean Ambrose won a six-man *Money in the Bank* Match to gain a future championship opportunity. He didn't wait long to cash in. That same night Ambrose took the WWE World Heavyweight Championship from Seth Rollins after Rollins won the Title from Roman Reigns.

# THE LUNATIC FRINGE
## — DEAN AMBROSE —

**THE UNPREDICTABLE STYLE** of Dean Ambrose has kept both friends and foes guessing ever since his WWE debut in 2012. In just a few short years, Dean Ambrose has managed to capture the WWE Championship, United States Championship, and Intercontinental Championship titles.

Mr. McMahon put Reigns's career on the line in a December 2015 WWE Championship Match. He defeated Sheamus to stay employed and become the new champ.

🏆 **TROPHY TRIVIA**

Roman Reigns was named Superstar of the Year at the 2014 Slammy Awards.

# ★ BEST-EVER...

## ▶ REIGNS VS. ALL MOMENTS

**★ RAW (June 16, 2014), Battle Royal**
Twenty Superstars entered the ring to battle for a single spot in the 2014 *Money in the Bank* Ladder Match, but only Reigns emerged victorious.

**★ Royal Rumble 2015**
After setting the record for eliminations the previous year, Reigns won the 30-man melee in his second attempt.

**★ RAW (January 11, 2016), 1 vs. All Match**
Faced with impossible odds, Roman Reigns beat 13 other Superstars and proved he cannot be intimidated.

## INFOMANIA

**DATE OF BIRTH:** May 25, 1985
**HEIGHT:** 6ft 3in (1.90m)
**WEIGHT:** 265lbs (120kg)
**HOMETOWN:** Pensacola, Florida
**SIGNATURE MOVE:** Superman Punch—a leaping right-hand punch to the jaw.
**DEBUT:** Reigns competed on NXT in October 2012 and defeated CJ Parker. Weeks later, at *Survivor Series 2012*, he emerged as part of The Shield stable and slammed Ryback through the announcer's table.

## WOW! 12

Number of Superstars Roman Reigns eliminated in one Royal Rumble Match in 2014—a WWE record.

## Q: WHO DID ROMAN REIGNS DEFEAT TO WIN HIS FIRST UNITED STATES CHAMPIONSHIP?

**A:** Rusev. After spoiling Rusev and Lana's wedding celebration by starting a tussle that resulted in Lana being covered with cake, Reigns delighted the WWE Universe further by taking the Title from Rusev at *Clash of Champions 2016*.

> ## "I'M NOT A GOOD GUY. I'M NOT A BAD GUY. I'M *THE* GUY!"
> ROMAN REIGNS

Reigns knocks the wind out of the 450lbs (204kg) Big Show with a thunderous Spear move.

## IN NUMBERS ● ● ●

**16** ➤ Number of Superstars in the 2015 tournament Reigns won at *Survivor Series* for his first WWE Championship

**15** ➤ Pay-per-view event wins since becoming a solo Superstar

**3** ➤ WWE Championship wins

**1** ➤ United States Championship win at *Clash of Champions 2016*

# THE BIG DOG
# — ROMAN REIGNS —

**TO ROMAN REIGNS**, every obstacle is just another opportunity to smash something to smithereens. Do not make the mistake of doubting this lean, agile powerhouse. Reigns is driven by proving people wrong. Tell him what he cannot do and you will soon learn that he can do it… and he will!

# LEADERBOARD

Highest number of Intercontinental Championship reigns.

| SUPERSTAR | NUMBER OF REIGNS |
|---|---|
| Chris Jericho | 9 |
| The Miz | 6 |
| Jeff Jarrett | 6 |
| Rob Van Dam | 6 |
| Wade Barrett | 5 |
| Dolph Ziggler | 5 |
| Triple H | 5 |

**Q: WHAT NICKNAME DID JERICHO GIVE HIMSELF DURING HIS RIVALRY WITH DEAN MALENKO, ALSO KNOWN AS THE MAN OF 1,000 HOLDS?**

**A:** The Man of 1,004 Holds.

## "YOU JUST MADE THE LIST!"

CHRIS JERICHO

Chris Jericho tries to force Seth Rollins to submit to his signature Walls of Jericho submission hold.

## WOW!

**11**

Number of different championships won (with a total of 29 separate reigns) across ECW, WCW, and WWE.

## 🏆 TROPHY TRIVIA

Chris Jericho won the Television Championship in both ECW (on June 22, 1996) and WCW (on August 10, 1998).

## AKA

Lionheart / The Ayatollah of Rock 'n' Rolla / Y2J

## CHAMPIONSHIP SCRAMBLE, *UNFORGIVEN* (SEPTEMBER 7, 2008)

Chris Jericho's first World Heavyweight Championship came in a Championship Scramble against Batista, Kane, Rey Mysterio and JBL—a 20-minute match with the last man to record a pin taking the title. When an injured CM Punk couldn't participate, Jericho took his spot and pinned Kane with only moments left to win the title.

### INFOMANIA

**DATE OF BIRTH:** November 9, 1970
**HEIGHT:** 6ft (1.82m)
**WEIGHT:** 227lbs (103kg)
**HOMETOWN:** Winnipeg, Canada
**SIGNATURE MOVE:** Walls of Jericho—Jericho sits on his opponent's back, grabs their legs, and pulls them backward.
**DEBUT:** Jericho interrupted The Rock's in-ring promo on an episode of *RAW* on August 9, 1999 to introduce himself to the WWE Universe.

# Y2J
## — CHRIS JERICHO —

**CHRIS JERICHO** has been a sports-entertainment mainstay since 1999. He has won dozens of championships around the world, including every major WWE title—the WWE Championship, World Heavyweight Championship, and the Tag Team Championship.

## WATCH OUT FOR OWENS!

Despite his gruff persona, it is impossible not to appreciate Owens for the action he delivers. His moves, which are both graceful and brutal, are a constant source of amazement to the WWE Universe.

### SUPERKICK
OWENS DRIVES HIS FOOT INTO A FOE'S CHEST WITH A MIGHTY KICK.

Kevin Owens battles Seth Rollins for the WWE Universal Championship.

### CANNONBALL
OWENS BOWLS INTO OPPONENTS AT SPEED WITH INCREDIBLE FORCE.

### POP-UP POWERBOMB
OWENS LAUNCHES HIS OPPONENTS HIGH, ONLY TO SLAM THEM DOWN.

### SUPER FISHERMAN BUSTER
TWISTING HIS OPPONENT ONTO THE MAT, OWENS DISPLAYS IMPRESSIVE AGILITY.

# THE PRIZEFIGHTER
## KEVIN OWENS

**KEVIN OWENS IS** brash, menacing, and brutal, and that is just when he talks! In the ring, few can match the variety of high-impact maneuvers Owens keeps at his disposal. This bad-tempered competitor is always looking for a fight. When he finds one, no Superstar can stand in his way.

**15** Number of years Owens spent competing around the world before getting a chance in WWE.

**DATE OF BIRTH:** May 7, 1984
**HEIGHT:** 6ft (1.83m)
**WEIGHT:** 266lbs (121kg)
**HOMETOWN:** Marieville, Canada
**SIGNATURE MOVE:** Pop-Up Powerbomb—Owens lifts his opponent up to shoulder height and then brings them crashing down onto the mat.
**DEBUT:** In a stunning upset, Kevin Owens defeated Superstar John Cena at *Elimination Chamber 2015*. He joined Carlito and John Laurinaitis as the only Superstars to beat Cena in their first WWE match. Out of the three, Owens was the only one who achieved the feat without resorting to foul play.

> **"WHEN I SAY I AM GOING TO DO SOMETHING, I DELIVER."**
> — KEVIN OWENS

## 🏆 TROPHY TRIVIA

Kevin Owens became the second WWE Universal Champion of all time when he prevailed in a Fatal 4-Way Elimination Match on *RAW*. Owens defeated Big Cass, Roman Reigns, and Seth Rollins.

## IN DETAIL

# KEVIN OWENS VS. SETH ROLLINS, *CLASH OF CHAMPIONS* (SEPTEMBER 22, 2016)

After becoming WWE Universal Champion, Kevin Owens boldly proclaimed that *RAW* was the "Kevin Owens Show." To back up his claims, Owens had to defeat former world champion Seth Rollins. Rollins was prepared for a fierce battle with Owens, but didn't expect Owens' best friend, Chris Jericho, to make an appearance. Owens attacked Seth's newly repaired knee, but Seth rebounded and hit his finisher move: the Pedigree. Jericho interfered with the match and left the referee incapacitated. But the referee recovered just in time to see Owens deliver his Pop-Up Powerbomb maneuver on Rollins, which ended the match.

## LEADERBOARD

Longest single reigns in the WWE Divas Championship

| SUPERSTAR | LENGTH OF REIGN |
|---|---|
| Nikki Bella | 301 days |
| AJ Lee | 295 days |
| Maryse | 212 days |
| Beth Phoenix | 204 days |
| Charlotte | 196 days (title was retired) |
| Michelle McCool | 159 days |
| Kaitlyn | 153 days |
| Layla | 140 days |
| Eve Torres | 120 days |
| Kelly Kelly | 104 days |

## Q: WHICH SIGNATURE MOVE OF HER FATHER'S DID CHARLOTTE ADAPT INTO HER OWN?

**A:** Figure-Four Leglock. Charlotte added a bridge to Ric Flair's move and created the Figure-Eight Leglock.

## IN DETAIL

## CHARLOTTE VS. NATALYA
## *NXT TAKEOVER* (MAY 29, 2014)

After the inaugural NXT Women's Champion, Paige, vacated the title when she joined *RAW*, an eight-woman tournament was held to crown a new champion. After beating Emma and Alexa Bliss in early rounds, Charlotte used her signature Natural Selection maneuver to pin Natalya and become the second NXT Women's Champion in WWE history.

**DATE OF BIRTH:** April 5, 1986
**HEIGHT:** 5ft 10in (1.78m)
**HOMETOWN:** Charlotte, North Carolina
**SIGNATURE MOVE:** Natural Selection—Charlotte leaps over her downed opponent and uses a facelock to drive them face-first into the mat.
**DEBUT:** Charlotte won a Triple Threat Match against Sasha Banks and Brie Bella at WWE *Battleground* on July 19, 2015.

At a Tag Team Match on WWE *RAW*, Charlotte reminds Bayley who is the queen of the *RAW* women's division by driving a knee into her opponent's back.

## 🏆 TROPHY TRIVIA

At the 2016 WWE Draft held on July 19 during *SmackDown*, Charlotte was a first-round pick and the third overall selection, making her the highest female chosen in that year's draft.

# THE QUEEN
## — CHARLOTTE —

**THE DAUGHTER OF** 16-time WWE Champion Ric Flair, Charlotte has continued to build on the Flair legacy. In a short space of time, Charlotte Flair has gained six championship reigns, including the NXT Women's Championship, the Divas Title, and four runs as the *RAW* Women's Champion.

61

**DATE OF BIRTH:** January 28, 1978
**HEIGHT:** 6ft 4in (1.93m)
**WEIGHT:** 267lbs (121kg)
**HOMETOWN:** Dublin, Ireland
**SIGNATURE MOVE:** White Noise—with brute strength, Sheamus drapes his foe over his back then leaps backward, slamming him into a pinning position.
**DEBUT:** Sheamus began competing for WWE's ECW brand in June 2009 when he defeated local competitor Oliver John in his first match.

### TITLE TRIVIA

Six months after his WWE debut, Sheamus won a Tables Match against John Cena, claiming the WWE Championship.

WOW! **18**

# THE CELTIC WARRIOR
## SHEAMUS

**A RUGGED BRAWLER** with roots tracing back to ancient Celtic warriors, Sheamus is a constant threat to anyone holding championship gold. Among other WWE titles, Sheamus has held the WWE Championship three times and the World Heavyweight Championship once.

## THE BEST BROGUE KICKS

Sheamus's Brogue Kick ranks among the most devastating moves in WWE. This simple maneuver, also known as a Bicycle Kick, has taken down several top Superstars and was briefly made illegal in 2012.

### WRESTLEMANIA XXVIII
THE BROGUE KICK CATCHES DANIEL BRYAN OFF GUARD.

### SURVIVOR SERIES 2015
SHEAMUS LEVELS AN UNSUSPECTING ROMAN REIGNS TO WIN THE TITLE.

### ROYAL RUMBLE 2012
THE SIGNATURE KICK ELIMINATES CHRIS JERICHO.

Sheamus inflicts pain on Cesaro with his Cloverleaf submission hold. These rivals later came together to become *RAW* Tag Team Champions.

## IN NUMBERS ●●●

**668** > Days as a champion in WWE

**5th** > Longest World Heavyweight Championship reign

**2nd** > Superstar to win *Royal Rumble*, *King of the Ring*, and *Money in the Bank*

**1st** > Irish-born WWE World Champion

**WOW!**
# 9

The number of years, out of his 11 competing in WWE, that The Miz has held a championship title.

## ★ BEST-EVER...
### MUST-SEE MIZ MOMENTS

**★ Stunt Double**
The Miz took his movie-star persona a step further by hiring Damien Sandow to be his stunt-double. Sandow soon changed his surname to "Mizdow."

**★ MizTV**
*MizTV*, The "Most Must-See Talk Show in WWE History," debuted on *RAW*. Over the years, The Miz has used his hosting gig to insult several of his rivals.

**★ Talkin' Smack**
The Miz lost his temper on the WWE Network talk show *Talkin' Smack* when *SmackDown Live* General Manager Daniel Bryan questioned his bravery inside the ring.

The Miz traps Dolph Ziggler in a Figure-Four Leglock—a punishing submission hold made famous by "Nature Boy" Ric Flair.

# THE AWESOME ONE
## THE MIZ

**THE MIZ IS** never short on words, and most of them are concerned with how awesome he is. But his impressive WWE resume makes it difficult to argue with any of his boasting. In over a decade, The Miz has won every title available to him and become a Hollywood movie star along the way.

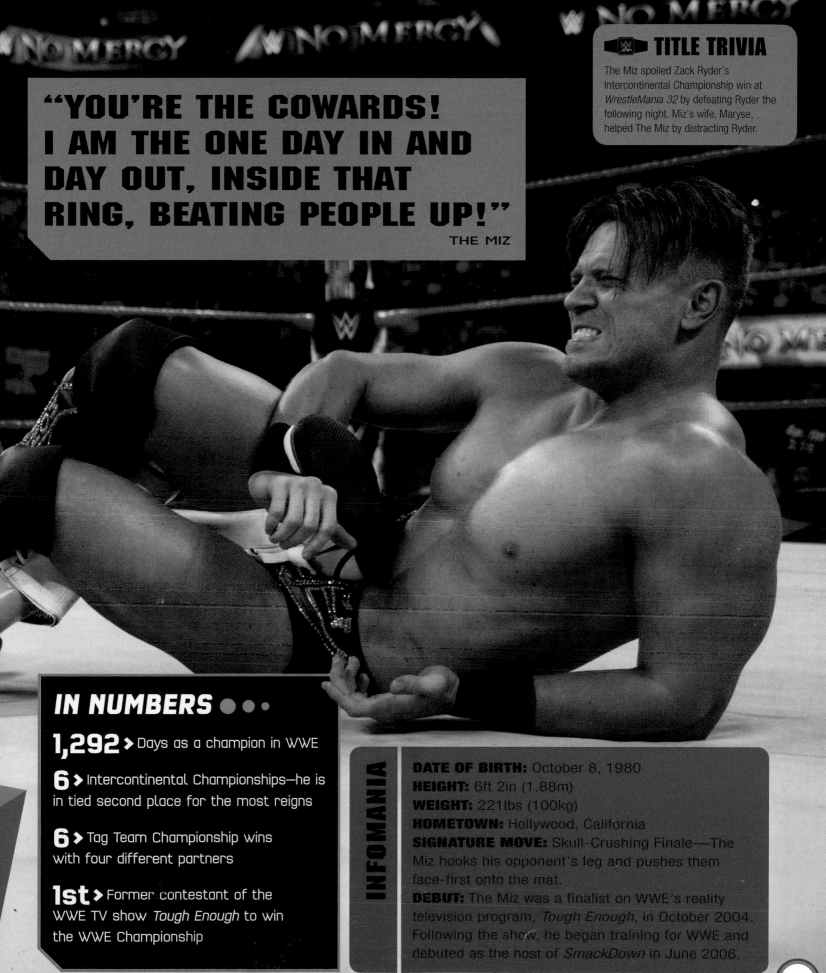

## "YOU'RE THE COWARDS! I AM THE ONE DAY IN AND DAY OUT, INSIDE THAT RING, BEATING PEOPLE UP!"

THE MIZ

### TITLE TRIVIA

The Miz spoiled Zack Ryder's Intercontinental Championship win at *WrestleMania 32* by defeating Ryder the following night. Miz's wife, Maryse, helped The Miz by distracting Ryder.

## IN NUMBERS ●●●

**1,292** ❯ Days as a champion in WWE

**6** ❯ Intercontinental Championships—he is in tied second place for the most reigns

**6** ❯ Tag Team Championship wins with four different partners

**1st** ❯ Former contestant of the WWE TV show *Tough Enough* to win the WWE Championship

### INFOMANIA

**DATE OF BIRTH:** October 8, 1980
**HEIGHT:** 6ft 2in (1.88m)
**WEIGHT:** 221lbs (100kg)
**HOMETOWN:** Hollywood, California
**SIGNATURE MOVE:** Skull-Crushing Finale—The Miz hooks his opponent's leg and pushes them face-first onto the mat.
**DEBUT:** The Miz was a finalist on WWE's reality television program, *Tough Enough*, in October 2004. Following the show, he began training for WWE and debuted as the host of *SmackDown* in June 2006.

Paul Wight / The Giant / The World's Largest Athlete

**TITLE TRIVIA**

As The Giant, Big Show debuted in WCW at *Halloween Havoc 1995* in Detroit, Michigan, defeating Hulk Hogan and becoming the youngest WCW Champion in history, age 23.

Big Show has been known to deliver stunning chest chops with his massive palms—as Ryback unfortunately found out at *SmackDown* in December 2014.

# THE WORLD'S LARGEST ATHLETE
## BIG SHOW

**ORIGINALLY BILLED AS** the son of André the Giant, Big Show has followed in his footsteps to become the most dominant big man in sports entertainment. As well as gaining seven world championships, Big Show has won no less than eight world tag team titles.

**DATE OF BIRTH:** February 8, 1972
**HEIGHT:** 7ft (2.13m)
**WEIGHT:** 383lbs (174kg)
**HOMETOWN:** Tampa, Florida
**SIGNATURE MOVE:** Weapon of Mass Destruction—a devastating K.O. punch.
**DEBUT:** Show broke through the ring to aid Mr. McMahon in a Steel Cage Match against Stone Cold Steve Austin at *In Your House: St. Valentine's Day Massacre* in February 1999.

## IN NUMBERS ● ● ●

**152** › Big Show's longest World Championship reign in days

**7** › Different championships won by Big Show: the WWE Title, World Heavyweight Championship, ECW Championship, Tag Team Championship, United States Championship, Intercontinental Championship, and Hardcore Championship

**3** › Different types of sports stars who have confronted Big Show at WrestleMania: sumo wrestler Akebono, boxer Floyd Mayweather, and NBA legend Shaquille O'Neal

## "NOBODY ROOTS FOR GOLIATH!"

BIG SHOW

## IN DETAIL

### TRIPLE H VS. THE ROCK VS. STONE COLD STEVE AUSTIN, *SURVIVOR SERIES* (NOVEMBER 14, 1999)

He wasn't even supposed to be in the title match, but an injury to Stone Cold Steve Austin created a title opportunity for Big Show, who earlier that night, won a Four-on-One *Survivor Series 1999* Elimination Match. Big Show choke-slammed Triple H and pinned him to win the WWE Championship.

## THE SHOWOFF THAT COULD

With Ziggler's skills, size is not required for rising to the top of WWE. Dolph was one of the last four men to hold the classic gold World Heavyweight Championship—proof that he could play with the big boys.

### SIZE CHART

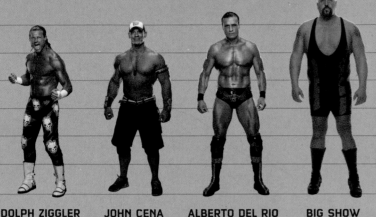

| DOLPH ZIGGLER | JOHN CENA | ALBERTO DEL RIO | BIG SHOW |
|---|---|---|---|
| 6ft (1.83m) | 6ft 1in (1.86m) | 6ft 5in (1.96m) | 7ft (2.13m) |

In a Title vs. Career Match at *No Mercy 2016*, Dolph Ziggler battles The Miz with both the Intercontinental Title and his WWE career at stake!

**WOW!**

## 121

Number of wins Dolph achieved in wrestling at Kent State University—a college record and a preview of things to come in WWE.

# THE SHOWOFF
## — DOLPH ZIGGLER —

**OFTEN UNDERESTIMATED BUT** never outperformed, Dolph Ziggler revels in bringing the WWE Universe to its feet. Racking up World Heavyweight, Intercontinental, and United States Championship reigns, Dolph's charisma and skill between the ropes make him a fan favorite.

**Q: WHO HAS ZIGGLER DEFEATED FOR BOTH THE INTERCONTINENTAL AND UNITED STATES CHAMPIONSHIPS?**

**A:** Kofi Kingston. Dolph won his first Intercontinental Championship from Kofi in August 2010. When the two high-tempo athletes met again at *Capital Punishment 2011*, Dolph used a Sleeper Hold to win Kofi's United States Championship.

## ★ BEST-EVER...

### ▶ SHOW-STEALING PERFORMANCES

★ **Survivor Series 2014 vs. Team Authority**
In a high-stakes Elimination Match, Ziggler was the last man standing for Team Cena, showing incredible guts. Dolph scored the winning pin on Seth Rollins.

★ **Hell in a Cell 2014 vs. Cesaro**
As the WWE Universe chanted "This is awesome!" Ziggler swept the powerful Cesaro two pinfalls to zero in a 2 out of 3 Falls Match.

★ **SummerSlam 2012 vs. Chris Jericho**
In a much-anticipated showdown, Dolph Ziggler and Chris Jericho blew the roof off the Staples Center, Los Angeles, in the opening match of WWE's Summer Spectacular.

★ **Bragging Rights 2010 vs. Daniel Bryan**
This fast-paced encounter ended in controversy. Dolph earned a three-count, but the referee deemed that Bryan's foot was on the ropes, disallowing the pinfall.

### TITLE TRIVIA

Dolph sent the *RAW* crowd into hysteria the night after *WrestleMania 29* when he used his Money in the Bank privilege to defeat Alberto Del Rio for the World Heavyweight Championship in 2013.

## INFOMANIA

**DATE OF BIRTH:** July 27, 1980
**HEIGHT:** 6ft (1.83m)
**WEIGHT:** 213lbs (97kg)
**HOMETOWN:** Cleveland, Ohio
**SIGNATURE MOVE:** Zig Zag—where an airborne Ziggler hooks his opponent under the chin and pulls him backward to the mat.
**DEBUT:** Dolph debuted as the caddy for Superstar golf fanatic Kerwin White in 2005. A year later, he reappeared as Nicky in the tag team Spirit Squad.

# ★ BEST-EVER...

## ▶ NXT WOMEN'S CHAMPIONSHIP MATCHES

**★ NXT TakeOver: Unstoppable (May 20, 2015) vs. Becky Lynch**
The Boss forced Becky Lynch to submit to the Bank Statement to retain her NXT Women's Championship.

**★ NXT TakeOver: Brooklyn (August 22, 2015) vs. Bayley**
In a bout many of the WWE Universe considered a match of the year, Sasha finally lost the NXT Women's Championship to her longtime nemesis, Bayley.

**★ NXT TakeOver: Respect (October 7, 2015) vs. Bayley**
Banks tried to regain the NXT Women's Championship from Bayley in a 30-Minute Iron Man Match for the title, but Bayley retained the Championship, three falls to two.

## TITLE TRIVIA

On July 25, 2016, Sasha Banks won her first *RAW* Women's Championship by pinning Charlotte on the first *RAW* episode after the 2016 WWE Draft.

# THE BOSS
## — SASHA BANKS —

**BRINGING AN** unmistakable charisma and style to both NXT and WWE rings, Sasha Banks has absolutely earned her nickname The Boss. She has only been a Superstar for a few years, but Banks has already achieved four championship reigns and continues to challenge her opponents.

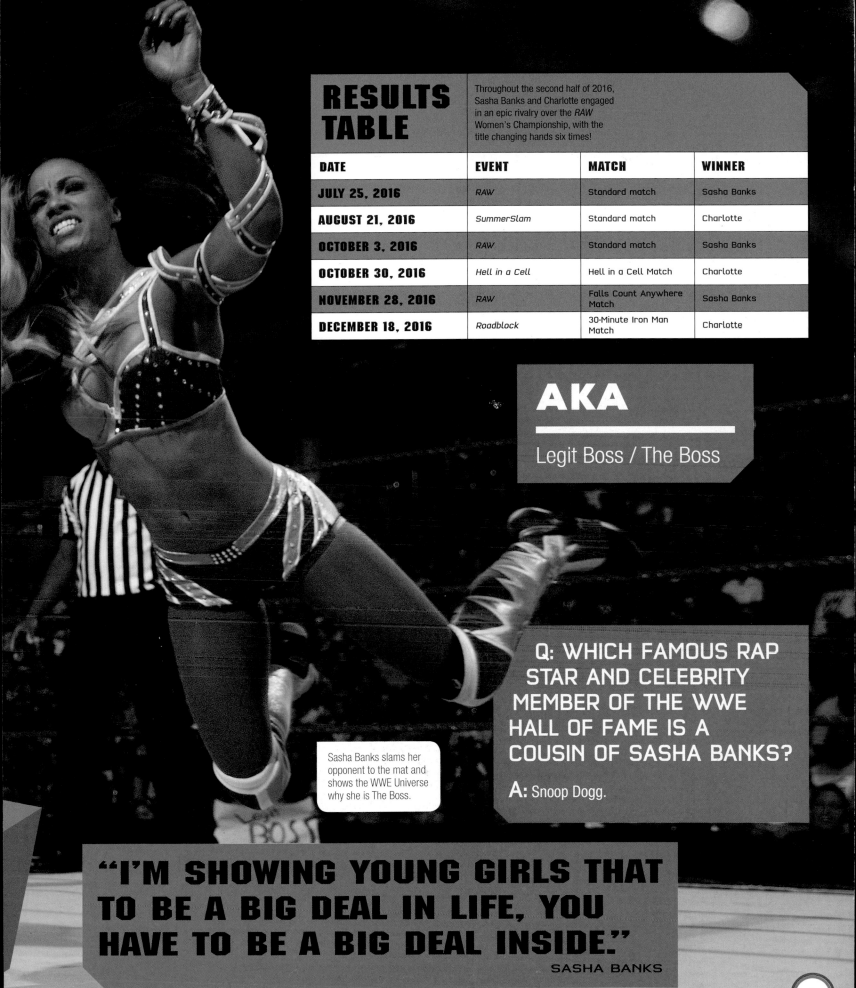

## RESULTS TABLE

Throughout the second half of 2016, Sasha Banks and Charlotte engaged in an epic rivalry over the *RAW* Women's Championship, with the title changing hands six times!

| DATE | EVENT | MATCH | WINNER |
|------|-------|-------|--------|
| JULY 25, 2016 | *RAW* | Standard match | Sasha Banks |
| AUGUST 21, 2016 | *SummerSlam* | Standard match | Charlotte |
| OCTOBER 3, 2016 | *RAW* | Standard match | Sasha Banks |
| OCTOBER 30, 2016 | *Hell in a Cell* | Hell in a Cell Match | Charlotte |
| NOVEMBER 28, 2016 | *RAW* | Falls Count Anywhere Match | Sasha Banks |
| DECEMBER 18, 2016 | *Roadblock* | 30-Minute Iron Man Match | Charlotte |

## AKA

Legit Boss / The Boss

Sasha Banks slams her opponent to the mat and shows the WWE Universe why she is The Boss.

Q: WHICH FAMOUS RAP STAR AND CELEBRITY MEMBER OF THE WWE HALL OF FAME IS A COUSIN OF SASHA BANKS?

A: Snoop Dogg.

## "I'M SHOWING YOUNG GIRLS THAT TO BE A BIG DEAL IN LIFE, YOU HAVE TO BE A BIG DEAL INSIDE."

SASHA BANKS

Bray Wyatt is a sinister Superstar whose quest is to instill fear into the WWE Universe. As well as his merciless brutality in the ring and creepy spider walk, Wyatt has the ability to brainwash others to join his "family" of followers.

## FAMILY BURIAL
KANE HAS BURIED HIS HALF-BROTHER, UNDERTAKER, ALIVE...TWICE!

## KANE'S DEVILISH DEEDS

No WWE Superstar has committed more carnage than Kane. For 20 years, Kane has proven why he is the "Devil's Favorite Demon."

## BURN, BROTHER, BURN
KANE SET FIRE TO A CASKET WITH UNDERTAKER INSIDE!

**DRAGGED TO HELL**
THE DEMON KANE DRAGGED SETH ROLLINS UNDER THE RING, WHICH THEN CAUGHT FIRE!

**SUPERSTAR SACRILEGE**
KANE DROPPED A PRIEST WITH A TOMBSTONE PILEDRIVER!

The Boogeyman consumed mouthfuls of live worms in the ring and often forced his opponents to partake!

Jake "The Snake" Roberts was known for preying on his rivals' fears. He once trapped "Macho Man" Randy Savage in the ring ropes while a cobra bit his arm!

If Bull Nakano's freakish face make-up was not terrifying enough, she would toss opponents across the ring by their hair and take pleasure in the pain it caused.

# SCARY SUPERSTARS

**NO MATTER** a Superstar's prowess in the ring, they'd be forgiven for checking under their bed to see if these frightful Superstars are lurking. Some, like Kane, chill the bones with their menacing presence, while others, like Jake "The Snake" Roberts, slither their way into an opponent's psyche.

Becky Lynch attempts to force Natalya to submit to her Dis-Arm-Her finisher move.

**WOW!**

**1** First woman selected by *SmackDown* during the 2016 WWE Draft, and the sixth contender to be selected overall.

# THE LASS KICKER
## BECKY LYNCH

**WHEN SHANE MCMAHON** and Daniel Bryan decided to build the *SmackDown* women's division at the 2016 WWE Draft, they made an astute choice by selecting Becky Lynch as the brand's cornerstone Superstar. She held the title for almost three months in late 2016.

**DATE OF BIRTH:** January 30, 1987
**HEIGHT:** 5ft 6in (1.68m)
**HOMETOWN:** Dublin, Ireland
**SIGNATURE MOVE:** The Dis-Arm-Her—Lynch pulls back her downed opponent's arm to force a submission.
**DEBUT:** Alongside partner Paige, Lynch lost a tag team match to Sasha Banks and Naomi on *RAW*, on July 20, 2015.

## "PEOPLE EXPECT US WOMEN TO STEAL THE SHOW AND WE HAVE TO LIVE UP TO IT!"

BECKY LYNCH

## IN DETAIL

### TABLES MATCH FOR THE *SMACKDOWN* WOMEN'S CHAMPIONSHIP, *WWE TLC 2016* (DECEMBER 4, 2016)

Becky Lynch defended her *SmackDown* Women's Championship against Alexa Bliss in the first Tables Match between female competitors for a championship. Lynch came close to winning the match on several occasions, almost putting Bliss through a table with an overhead suplex and a slam. However, Bliss shocked the champion and stole the Title with a timely Powerbomb onto a table placed outside the ring.

Q: WHICH *RAW* SUPERSTAR DID LYNCH ELIMINATE AT THE *SURVIVOR SERIES 2016 RAW* VS. *SMACKDOWN* WOMEN'S ELIMINATION MATCH?

**A:** Nia Jax.

WOW!

# 51

Number of wins Rusev had during the undefeated streak that began his WWE career.

## RAW SUPERSTARS TO WATCH OUT FOR

**Sami Zayn:** This fearless, scrappy competitor is well versed in several wrestling styles.

**Neville:** Nicknamed "The Man that Gravity Forgot," this wrestler can soar above the ring.

**Darren Young:** With WWE legend Bob Backlund guiding him, Young is destined for greatness.

**Finn Balor:** Nicknamed "The Demon King," this captivating Superstar could be big in WWE.

**Sin Cara:** This masked Superstar thrills audiences with his high-flying escapades.

## THE NEW FACE OF DESTRUCTION

Braun Strowman's fearsome demeanor and staggering proportions make him one of WWE's most intimidating Superstars. He rises above these other formidable competitors.

### SIZE CHART

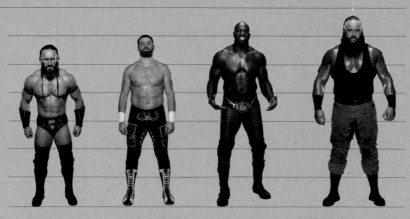

| NEVILLE | SAMI ZAYN | TITUS O'NEIL | BRAUN STROWMAN |
|---------|-----------|--------------|----------------|
| 5ft 8in (1.72m) | 6ft 1in (1.85m) | 6ft 6in (1.98m) | 6ft 8in (2.03m) |

Rusev's Accolade submission hold has caused opponents to scream for mercy or pass out in pain.

## HISTORIC SLAM
CESARO SLAMS 425LBS (193KG) BIG SHOW TO WIN AT WRESTLEMANIA 30.

## CESARO'S STRENGTH

Cesaro might be the most well-rounded Superstar in WWE. He has the strength to hoist Superstars twice his size and the stamina to swing them in circles for over a minute. These amazing skills have made him so popular, fans organize a "Cesaro Section" in every arena hoping to rally him toward further success in WWE.

## GUT-WRENCHING POWER
CESARO LIFTS BIG E UP AND OVER HIS HEAD FOR A GUTWRENCH SUPLEX.

## STRONGMAN NEUTRALIZED
CESARO PICKED UP THE 412LBS (187KG) MARK HENRY FOR A NEUTRALIZER.

## SWING SENSATION
CESARO SWING ROUND 7FT 1IN (2.16M) GREAT KHALI.

## "IF YOU FACE ME, I WILL CRUSH YOU!"
RUSEV

# RAW SUPERSTARS

From high-flying cruiserweights to hulking monsters, RAW Superstars must be ready for anything. Strongmen like Cesaro, Rusev, and Braun Strowman use their mountainous muscle to overpower their foes, while fierce competitors like Sami Zayn and Finn Bálor unleash a flurry of offensive firepower.

Apollo Crews is just as dangerous above the ropes as he is between them. He has an impressive aerial assault and jaw-dropping muscle power to match!

## 🏆 TROPHY TRIVIA

Kalisto took home the 2015 Slammy Award for Shocking Moment of the Year for executing his signature move, Salida Del Sol, from the top of a 15-foot (4.6-m) ladder!

WOW! **301**

Number of days Nikki Bella held the (now retired) Divas Championship— a WWE record.

# SMACKDOWN LIVE STANDOUTS

**AS SMACKDOWN LIVE** approaches its 20th anniversary, the action is more intense than ever. With the emergence of exciting young Superstars such as Apollo Crews, Alexa Bliss, and Baron Corbin, anyone holding a championship had best bring their A-game to the show every Tuesday night.

Kalisto baffles opponents twice his size with an endless supply of creative moves performed at warp speed.

## "I AM HERE TO SHOCK THE WORLD."
KALISTO

**★ Alexa Bliss's fight match (February 21, 2017)**
Alexa Bliss became the first two-time *SmackDown* Women's Champion by beating the Superstar she defeated for her first title, Becky Lynch. Up to her usual tricks, Bliss pinned Lynch by clutching her tights out of view of the referee.

**★ Naomi's Elimination Chamber (February 12, 2017)**
In 2016, Naomi unveiled a flashy new look and with it, a renewed determination to reach the apex of *SmackDown Live*'s women's division. Her hard work finally paid off at *Elimination Chamber*, when she defeated Alexa Bliss to capture the first title of her seven-year career. During the celebration, the WWE Universe chanted, "You deserve it."

**★ Luke Harper's near miss (February 21, 2017)**
After spending nearly his entire WWE career serving Bray Wyatt's agenda, Harper went solo in 2017 and almost instantly earned a spot in the main event of *WrestleMania*. Only Harper and AJ Styles remained in a 10-Superstar Battle Royal Match. The match ended in a draw when both Superstars fell over the ropes onto the floor at the same time.

## SMACKDOWN LIVE SUPERSTARS TO WATCH

**Baron Corbin:** A self-proclaimed "Lone Wolf," this callous Superstar is out to destroy anyone in his path.

**Erick Rowan:** With his grisly appearance and hulking size, Rowan is a threatening presence in the ring.

**Carmella:** Since joining *SmackDown Live* in 2016, Carmella has backed up her tough talk and proven to be equal parts dangerous and fabulous.

Nikki Bella was blindsided by a mystery attacker who turned out to be her friend Natalya. The Superstars concluded their rivalry on *SmackDown Live* in a Falls Count Anywhere Match, won by Natalya.

## PAUL HEYMAN'S GUYS

During his admirable WWE managerial career, Paul Heyman has been by the side of numerous world champions.

### BROCK LESNAR

HEYMAN LED LESNAR WHEN HE ENDED THE UNDERTAKER'S WINNING STREAK AND BECAME WWE CHAMPION.

### BIG SHOW

HEYMAN BETRAYED BROCK LESNAR TO HELP BIG SHOW WIN THE WWE CHAMPIONSHIP AT THE 2002 SURVIVOR SERIES.

### CM PUNK

HEYMAN MANAGED CM PUNK DURING HIS HISTORIC WWE CHAMPIONSHIP REIGN.

### KURT ANGLE

HEYMAN ADVISED KURT ANGLE WHILE THE OLYMPIC HERO WAS WWE CHAMPION AND EVEN CREATED THE TAG TEAM "TEAM ANGLE" IN HIS HONOR.

## "OHHH YESSS!"

PAUL BEARER

# 846

Combined weight in pounds (384kg) of the Natural Disasters when Jimmy Hart guided them to the WWE Tag Team Championship.

## ★ BEST-EVER...

### ▶ MANAGERIAL ASSISTS

**★ WrestleMania V, Bobby Heenan's Leg-Up**
When Rick Rude attempted to pin the Ultimate Warrior for the Intercontinental Championship, Bobby Heenan sneakily held on to the Warrior's leg, preventing a kick-out and allowing Rude to win the title.

**★ Backlash 2016, Maryse's Distraction**
Maryse ensured that her client and husband, The Miz, continued his Intercontinental Championship reign by distracting challenger Dolph Ziggler just enough for The Miz to pin him.

**★ King of the Ring 1998, Paul Bearer's Blood-red Suit**
Paul Bearer cleverly got his client Kane in a First-Blood Match for the WWE Championship against reigning champion Stone Cold Steve Austin. With Kane dressed in a red suit with a mask to match, it was much easier to see Austin bleed, so Kane won his first World Championship.

## 🏆 TROPHY TRIVIA

In 1987, Bobby Heenan, Jimmy Hart, Slick, and Mr. Fuji were four nominees for the Slammy Award "Manager of the Year." The winner was: "None of the Above!"

For years, Paul Bearer accompanied Undertaker to the ring, often holding the mysterious urn that was said to be the source of The Deadman's immense power.

# SUPERSTAR MANAGERS

**A GOOD MANAGER** remains by a Superstar's side as they battle their biggest competitors. Some managers help their charges by providing extra training or strategy advice, while others use their time at the ringside to find ways to bend the rules and give a Superstar the extra edge in a match.

Lince Dorado and Mustafa Ali trade awe-inspiring maneuvers during the cruiserweight Superstars' debuts on WWE's *205 Live*.

WOW!

**10**

Number of countries that are represented in WWE's cruiserweight roster, including the UK, India, Japan, and Mexico.

# CRUISERWEIGHTS

**WWE'S CRUISERWEIGHTS DELIVER** explosive action each week on *RAW* and on their own dedicated show, *205 Live*. Featuring Superstars weighing 205lbs (93kg) or less, these world-class competitors clash at a blistering pace that is guaranteed to thrill and excite the WWE Universe.

Cruiserweight Classic winner TJ Perkins battles veteran Superstar Brian Kendrick at WWE *Clash of Champions 2016.*

# ★ BEST-EVER...

## 205 LIVE CRUISERWEIGHT DRAMAS

**★ Kendrick's Comeback (December 12, 2014)**
Former Tag Team Champion Brian Kendrick returned to WWE after a seven-year hiatus. After a strong showing in the Cruiserweight Classic, he stayed with WWE and won the Cruiserweight Championship at *Hell in a Cell 2016.*

**★ Historic Debut (November 29, 2016)**
On the debut episode of *205 Live*, "The Outlandish" Rich Swann stole the show by defeating Brian Kendrick for the Cruiserweight Championship.

**★ The Extraordinary Gentleman (November–December, 2016)**
Despite his gentlemanly appearance, James Gallagher is a dangerous man. The Superstar picked up consecutive victories against Ariya Daivari to begin his *205 Live* career and followed this up with an impressive win over Drew Gulak.

## FLYIN' BRIAN
BRIAN PILLMAN WON A TOURNAMENT IN OCTOBER 1991 TO BECOME WCW'S INAUGURAL CRUISERWEIGHT CHAMPION.

## PINT-SIZED POWER
IN JULY 2007, THE 4FT 5IN (1.35M) HORNSWOGGLE CLAIMED THE CRUISERWEIGHT CHAMPIONSHIP. THE TITLE WAS RETIRED TWO MONTHS LATER.

## HELMS DOMINATES
GREGORY HELMS (TOP RIGHT) WON THE CRUISERWEIGHT CHAMPIONSHIP AT *ROYAL RUMBLE 2006* AND HELD IT FOR 385 DAYS.

## CRUISERWEIGHT HISTORY

The original Cruiserweight Championship was introduced in WCW and was contested in WWE from 2001 to 2007. A decade later, WWE's new era of cruiserweights is determined to build on the legacy of these originals.

# CHAMPIONSHIPS

03

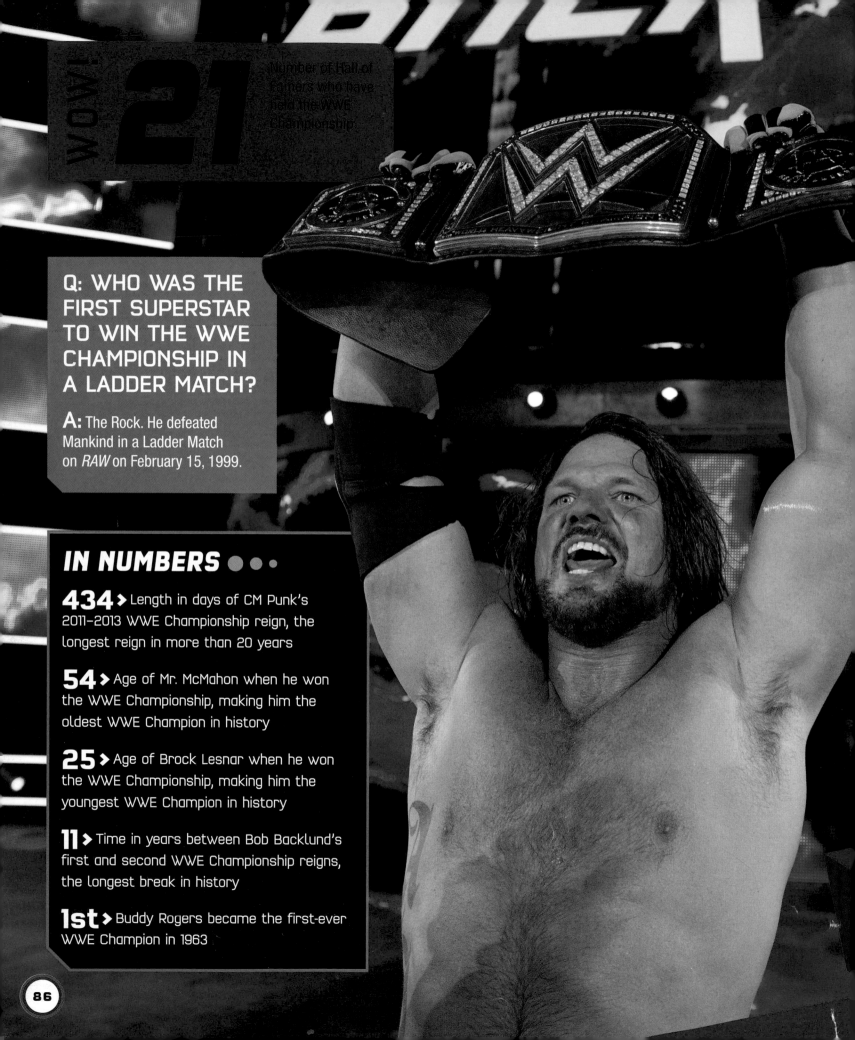

# 21

Number of Hall of Famers who have held the WWE Championship.

## Q: WHO WAS THE FIRST SUPERSTAR TO WIN THE WWE CHAMPIONSHIP IN A LADDER MATCH?

**A:** The Rock. He defeated Mankind in a Ladder Match on *RAW* on February 15, 1999.

## IN NUMBERS ● ● ●

**434 >** Length in days of CM Punk's 2011–2013 WWE Championship reign, the longest reign in more than 20 years

**54 >** Age of Mr. McMahon when he won the WWE Championship, making him the oldest WWE Champion in history

**25 >** Age of Brock Lesnar when he won the WWE Championship, making him the youngest WWE Champion in history

**11 >** Time in years between Bob Backlund's first and second WWE Championship reigns, the longest break in history

**1st >** Buddy Rogers became the first-ever WWE Champion in 1963

AJ Styles capped off an incredible first year in WWE by capturing the WWE Championship from Dean Ambrose at *Backlash 2016*.

## FATAL 4-WAY, IN YOUR HOUSE 13 (FEBRUARY 16, 1997)

When Shawn Michaels had to relinquish the WWE Championship due to a knee injury, a Fatal 4-Way Match was held at *In Your House 13: Final Four* to crown a new champion. Bret "Hit Man" Hart outlasted Vader, Stone Cold Steve Austin, and Undertaker to win the WWE Championship for the fourth time in his career.

# RESULTS TABLE

Third time's the charm: the first seven Superstars to win a third WWE Championship and when they claimed them.

| SUPERSTAR | DATE | OPPONENT | EVENT |
|-----------|------|----------|-------|
| HULK HOGAN | March 24, 1991 | Sgt. Slaughter | *WrestleMania VII* |
| BRET "HIT MAN" HART | November 19, 1995 | Diesel | *Survivor Series* |
| SHAWN MICHAELS | November 9, 1997 | Bret "Hit Man" Hart | *Survivor Series* |
| THE ROCK | February 15, 1999 | Mankind | *RAW* |
| STONE COLD STEVE AUSTIN | March 28, 1999 | The Rock | *WrestleMania XV* |
| UNDERTAKER | May 23, 1999 | Stone Cold Steve Austin | *Over The Edge* |
| MANKIND | August 22, 1999 | Stone Cold Steve Austin | *SummerSlam* |

## TITLE TRIVIA

Stan Stasiak defeated Pedro Morales for the WWE Championship on September 1, 1973 in Philadelphia, Pennsylvania— the first time the title changed hands outside of New York City.

## "I WILL FIGHT LIKE MY LIFE DEPENDS ON IT... BECAUSE IT DOES."

TRIPLE H PRIOR TO HIS WWE CHAMPIONSHIP MATCH AT *WRESTLEMANIA XXIV*

# WWE CHAMPIONSHIP

**IT'S THE RICHEST PRIZE** in sports entertainment, and winning it even once cements the legacy of a Superstar. For more than five decades, competitors from the farthest corners of the Earth have traveled to WWE to attempt to capture the WWE Championship.

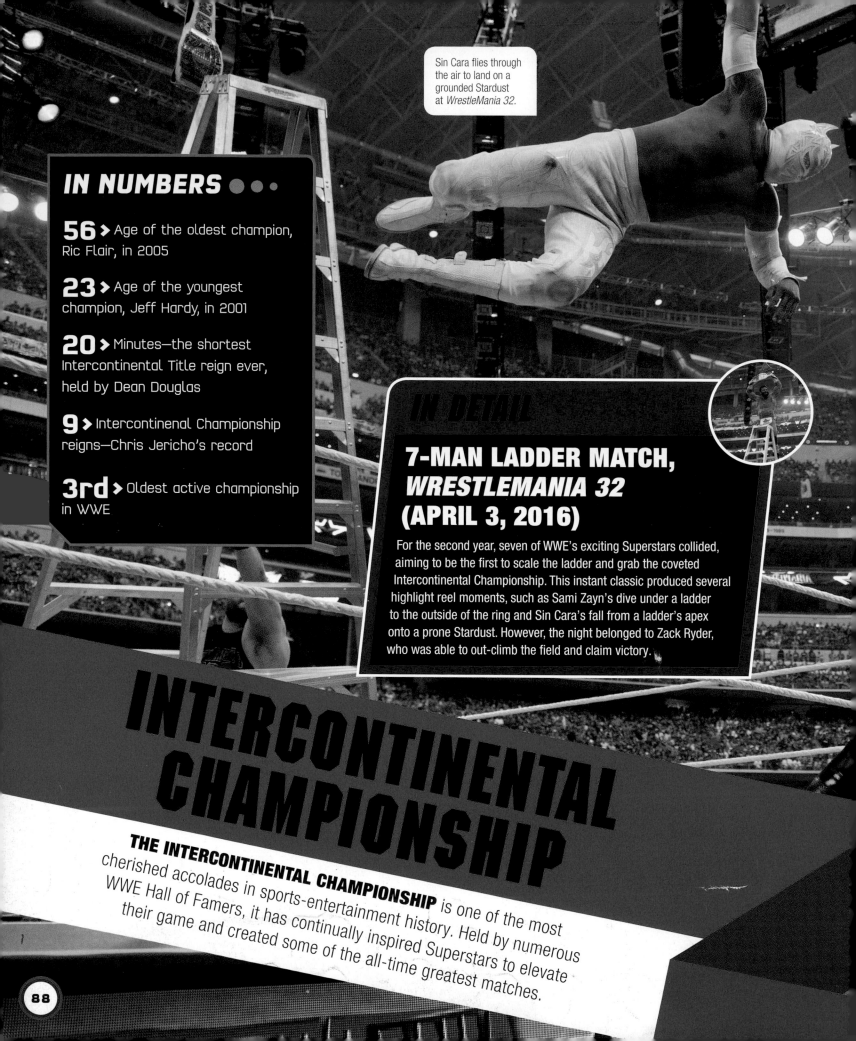

Sin Cara flies through the air to land on a grounded Stardust at *WrestleMania 32*.

## IN NUMBERS ●●●

**56** ❯ Age of the oldest champion, Ric Flair, in 2005

**23** ❯ Age of the youngest champion, Jeff Hardy, in 2001

**20** ❯ Minutes—the shortest Intercontinental Title reign ever, held by Dean Douglas

**9** ❯ Intercontinenal Championship reigns—Chris Jericho's record

**3rd** ❯ Oldest active championship in WWE

## IN DETAIL

### 7-MAN LADDER MATCH, *WRESTLEMANIA 32* (APRIL 3, 2016)

For the second year, seven of WWE's exciting Superstars collided, aiming to be the first to scale the ladder and grab the coveted Intercontinental Championship. This instant classic produced several highlight reel moments, such as Sami Zayn's dive under a ladder to the outside of the ring and Sin Cara's fall from a ladder's apex onto a prone Stardust. However, the night belonged to Zack Ryder, who was able to out-climb the field and claim victory.

# INTERCONTINENTAL CHAMPIONSHIP

**THE INTERCONTINENTAL CHAMPIONSHIP** is one of the most cherished accolades in sports-entertainment history. Held by numerous WWE Hall of Famers, it has continually inspired Superstars to elevate their game and created some of the all-time greatest matches.

## ORIGINAL

THE INAUGURAL INTERCONTINENTAL CHAMPION PAT PATTERSON WORE THIS RED LEATHER STRAP TITLE.

## 1980S STYLE

RANDY "MACHO MAN" SAVAGE HELD THIS POPULAR VERSION IN 1986.

## TITLE STYLES

The Intercontinental Championship Title was introduced to WWE in 1979. Since then, the title's look and style has evolved to reflect the times while still preserving its time-honored prestige.

## THE MOST ENDURING

SHELTON BENJAMIN HELD THE INTERCONTINENTAL CHAMPIONSHIP'S LONGEST-RUNNING DESIGN.

## "WINNING THIS TITLE DIDN'T JUST CHANGE MY CAREER. IT CHANGED MY LIFE."

DOLPH ZIGGLER

## IN LIVING COLOR

ULTIMATE WARRIOR UNVEILED MANY DIFFERENT COLORS FROM 1989 TO 1990.

LADDER MATCH

## WHITE OUT

CODY RHODES BROUGHT BACK THE WHITE LOOK SIMILAR TO THE CLASSIC SHAWN MICHAELS VERSION.

## WOW! 454

Number of days of Honky Tonk Man's record Intercontinental Championship reign from June 1987 to August 1988.

**Q: WHICH POP STAR WAS IN WENDI RICHTER'S CORNER WHEN SHE WON THE WOMEN'S CHAMPIONSHIP AT THE FIRST *WRESTLEMANIA* IN 1985?**

**A:** Cyndi Lauper.

Introduced at *WrestleMania 32*, the *RAW* Women's Championship title has been the subject of epic battles.

## WOW! 28

Number of consecutive years that the Fabulous Moolah held the Women's Championship—the longest continuous reign of any WWE title in history.

## IN NUMBERS ●●●

**408** ➤ The record number of days for which AJ Lee held the Divas Championship

**76** ➤ Age of the Fabulous Moolah when she won her last Women's Championship, making her the oldest champion in history

**21** ➤ Age of Paige when she won the WWE Divas Championship, making her the youngest champion in history

**4** ➤ Number of times Charlotte Flair held the *RAW* Women's Championship in 2016

## LEADERBOARD

Longest Women's Championship reigns by Superstars who only held the title once.

| SUPERSTAR | DAYS TITLE WAS HELD | YEAR WON |
|---|---|---|
| Rockin' Robin | 502 | 1988 |
| Sensational Sherri | 441 | 1987 |
| Chyna | 214 | 2001 |
| Sable | 176 | 1998 |
| Stephanie McMahon | 146 | 2000 |
| Bull Nakano | 134 | 1994 |

## BETH PHOENIX
THREE-TIME WOMEN'S CHAMPION AND ONE-TIME DIVAS CHAMPION.

**MICHELLE MCCOOL**
TWO-TIME WOMEN'S CHAMPION AND TWO-TIME DIVAS CHAMPION.

## MELINA
THREE-TIME WOMEN'S CHAMPION AND TWO-TIME DIVAS CHAMPION.

## IN DETAIL

### LUMBERJILL MATCH, NIGHT OF CHAMPIONS (SEPTEMBER 19, 2010)

Michelle McCool (and her LayCool tag team partner, Layla) had successfully defended the Women's Title on *SmackDown* for months, so they decided to target Melina's Divas Championship in a championship unification match. Despite the Lumberjill match stipulation that all the female Superstars surrounding the ring cannot interfere, Layla managed to help her partner defeat Melina and claim both titles.

**MICKIE JAMES**
FIVE-TIME WOMEN'S CHAMPION AND ONE-TIME DIVAS CHAMPION.

### TITLE TRIVIA

On January 31, 2000, Hervina defeated the Kat for the Women's Championship. But Hervina was really Harvey Wippleman in disguise, making him the only man to win the Women's Championship!

# WOMEN'S CHAMPIONSHIP

**FIRST INTRODUCED** in 1956, the Women's Championship is older than the WWE title by seven years. The championship has been claimed by some of the greatest female Superstars in sports entertainment history, as has the WWE Divas Championship, which ran from 2008 to 2016.

## UNIVERSAL CHAOS

The era of the WWE Universal Championship got off to an eventful start in August 2016. During the first eight days of the Title's existence, two new Champions were crowned.

## Q: WHO IS THE WWE UNIVERSAL CHAMPIONSHIP NAMED AFTER?

**A:** Everyone—the passionate members of the WWE Universe! Stephanie McMahon and Mick Foley announced its creation on the July 25, 2016 episode of *RAW*. Stephanie made it clear that the WWE Universe had demanded another World Title alongside the WWE Championship, and that is what they got.

### SUMMERSLAM (AUGUST 21, 2016)
FINN BÁLOR DEFEATED SETH ROLLINS TO BECOME THE INAUGURAL WWE UNIVERSAL CHAMPION.

### RAW (AUGUST 22, 2016)
ROMAN REIGNS, KEVIN OWENS, SETH ROLLINS, AND BIG CASS EACH WON MATCHES TO CONTEND FOR THE TITLE.

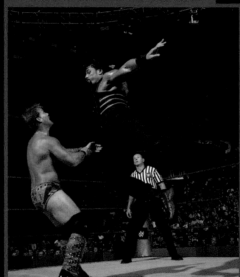

### RAW (AUGUST 29, 2016)
KEVIN OWENS WON A FATAL 4-WAY MATCH TO BECOME THE NEW CHAMPION.

### RAW (AUGUST 22, 2016)
FINN BÁLOR GAVE UP THE WWE UNIVERSAL CHAMPIONSHIP DUE TO AN INJURY.

## IN DETAIL

### FINN BÁLOR VS. SETH ROLLINS, *SUMMERSLAM* (AUGUST 21, 2016)

In just his third WWE match, Finn Bálor battled Seth Rollins for the first WWE Universal Championship. Bálor unleashed his "Demon King" persona for the bout, covering himself in body paint. Not intimidated, Rollins launched Bálor into the barricade with a Powerbomb and later flattened him with his Pedigree finisher. Showing great determination, Bálor refused to be pinned. Instead, he countered Seth's next Pedigree attempt, setting up his own finishing move, the Coup de Grace, to pin Rollins and claim *RAW's* top prize.

The WWE Universal Championship title features a red leather strap with a shimmering WWE logo on its faceplate.

# WWE UNIVERSAL CHAMPIONSHIP

**WHEN THE WWE CHAMPIONSHIP** became property of *SmackDown Live* in 2016, *RAW* Commissioner Stephanie McMahon and General Manager Mick Foley introduced the WWE Universal Championship. It is now the most celebrated prize for Superstars competing on the *RAW* brand.

# LEADERBOARD
Most United States Championship reigns.

## LEADERBOARD
Most United States Championship reigns.

| SUPERSTAR | NUMBER OF TITLE REIGNS |
|---|---|
| Ric Flair | 6 |
| Lex Luger | 5 |
| John Cena | 5 |
| Chris Benoit | 5 |
| Wahoo McDaniel | 5 |
| Bret "Hit Man" Hart | 5 |
| Blackjack Mulligan | 4 |
| Booker T | 4 |
| Ricky Steamboat | 4 |

## WOW!

# 84

Number of Superstars who have held the United States Championship over its history, including 25 future WWE Hall of Famers.

Roman Reigns won his first United States Championship at *Night of Champions 2016* and held the Title for four months.

# UNITED STATES CHAMPIONSHIP

**THE UNITED STATES CHAMPIONSHIP** is the second-oldest active title after the WWE Championship. It has been a much sought-after title for more than four decades, first in Mid-Atlantic Championship Wrestling, and then NWA, WCW, and, for the past decade and a half, WWE.

# IN NUMBERS ● ● ●

**950 ›** Record number of days the United States Championship was held by Lex Luger

**3 ›** WWE brands that have been the exclusive home of the United States Championship: *RAW*, *SmackDown*, and *ECW*

**2 ›** Superstars that simultaneously held the United States Championship and a World Title—Booker T (WCW title) and Seth Rollins (WWE title)

**1 ›** Total number of days Raven held the United States Championship

# IN DETAIL

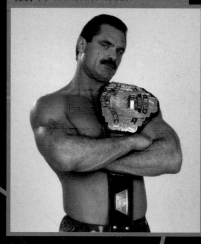

## BIG SHOW VS. JOHN CENA, WRESTLEMANIA XX (MARCH 14, 2004)

The opening match at *WrestleMania XX* featured Big Show defending the United States Championship against John Cena. The match was historic for several reasons: it was the first time the Title was ever defended on the grand stage of *WrestleMania*, and when Cena defeated the giant Show, he captured the first championship of his incredible WWE career.

### TITLE TRIVIA

On January 1, 1975, Harley Race defeated Johnny Weaver in the finals of a tournament to crown the first-ever United States Champion. Race would go on to hold the title for six months.

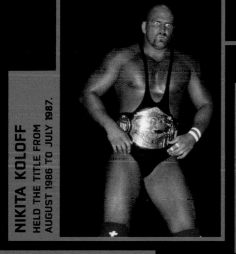

**NIKITA KOLOFF**
HELD THE TITLE FROM AUGUST 1986 TO JULY 1987.

**DEAN AMBROSE**
HELD THE TITLE FROM MAY 2013 TO MAY 2014.

**RICK RUDE**
HELD THE TITLE FROM NOVEMBER 1991 TO JANUARY 1993.

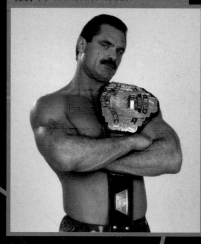

**MVP**
HELD THE TITLE FROM MAY 2007 TO APRIL 2008.

**LEX LUGER**
HELD THE TITLE FROM MAY 1989 TO OCTOBER 1990.

## THE FIVE MEMBERS OF THE 300 CLUB

In its history, only five Superstars have ever managed to hold the United States Championship for more than 300 consecutive days.

**A:** Tyson Kidd and Cesaro. The New Day trio invoked WWE's "Freebird Rule," at *Extreme Rules 2015* following the win. The rule allows any two members of a team of three to defend the titles. Ironically, it was Cesaro and his new partner, Sheamus, who ended The New Day's second reign.

## IN NUMBERS ● ● ●

**483** ❯ Number of days The New Day held the Tag Team Championship for—the longest in WWE history

**10** ❯ The most Tag Team Championship reigns in WWE history, set by The Dudley Boyz

**5** ❯ Minutes—the length of John Cena and The Miz's record for the shortest Tag Team Championship reign

Luke Gallows and Karl Anderson celebrate after winning the *RAW* Tag Team Titles at *Royal Rumble 2017*.

# TAG TEAM CHAMPIONSHIP

**IN WWE**, the combined strength of two or more Superstars is often the catalyst for energetic and entertaining in-ring action. For 45 years, the toughest pairings have contested WWE's prized Tag Team Championships. Today, both *RAW* and *SmackDown Live* feature their own exclusive titles.

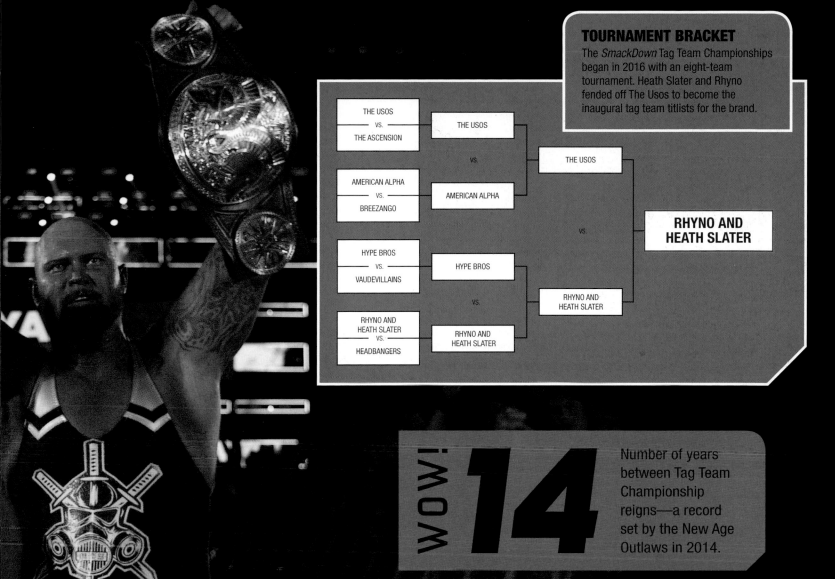

## TOURNAMENT BRACKET

The *SmackDown* Tag Team Championships began in 2016 with an eight-team tournament. Heath Slater and Rhyno fended off The Usos to become the inaugural tag team titlists for the brand.

THE USOS
VS.
THE ASCENSION

THE USOS

AMERICAN ALPHA
VS.
BREEZANGO

AMERICAN ALPHA

VS.

THE USOS

HYPE BROS
VS.
VAUDEVILLAINS

HYPE BROS

RHYNO AND
HEATH SLATER
VS.
HEADBANGERS

RHYNO AND
HEATH SLATER

VS.

THE USOS

VS.

RHYNO AND
HEATH SLATER

**RHYNO AND
HEATH SLATER**

## WOW! 14

Number of years between Tag Team Championship reigns—a record set by the New Age Outlaws in 2014.

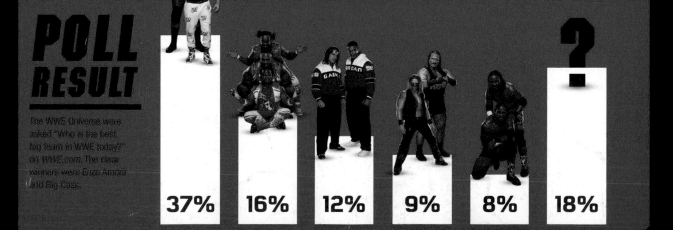

## POLL RESULT

The WWE Universe were asked "Who is the best tag team in WWE today?" on *WWE.com*. The clear winners were Enzo Amore and Big Cass.

| 37% | 16% | 12% | 9% | 8% | 18% |
|---|---|---|---|---|---|
| Enzo Amore and Big Cass | The New Day | American Alpha | Rhyno and Heath Slater | The Usos | Other |

# 100

Number of Superstars that have won a *King of the Ring* match (at any phase of the tournament) between 1985 and 2016.

## TITLE TRIVIA

On July 8, 1985, Don Muraco pinned the Iron Sheik to win a 16-man tournament and be crowned the first *King of the Ring* in Foxboro, Massachusetts.

**ROUND OF 32**
DEFEATED BRADSHAW.

King Booker beat Rey Mysterio to win the World Heavyweight Championship just a few months after winning the 2006 *King of the Ring* tournament.

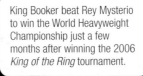

**ROUND OF 16**
DEFEATED BUBBA RAY DUDLEY.

**QUARTERFINALS**
DEFEATED CHRIS JERICHO.

## Q: WHO IS THE ONLY WOMAN TO WIN A *KING OF THE RING* MATCH?

**A:** Chyna. She gained victories in the 1999 and 2000 *King of the Ring* tournaments.

**SEMIFINALS**
DEFEATED CRASH HOLLY.

## KING KURT

Generally, the *King of the Ring* tournament has eight or 16 participants, but in 2000, 32 Superstars competed for the Title. The eventual Champion, Kurt Angle, had to win five matches—the most in a single year.

**FINALS**
DEFEATED RIKISHI.

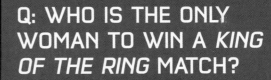

## BAD NEWS BARRETT VS. NEVILLE, *KING OF THE RING 2015*

After a five-year absence, the *King of the Ring* tournament returned to WWE in 2015. The finals pitted the former leader of the Nexus, Bad News Barrett, against the man that gravity forgot, Neville. Barrett was able to use his strength and power to overwhelm the WWE rookie and claim the title, making him the third consecutive European Superstar to win *King of the Ring*, after William Regal and Sheamus.

## "BOW DOWN TO KING BOOKER!"

JERRY LAWLER, AFTER BOOKER T WAS CROWNED THE 2006 *KING OF THE RING*

# KING OF THE RING

**SINCE 1985**, wrestling royalty has been crowned in 20 different *King of the Ring* tournaments, in which Superstars have had to beat between three and five other Superstars. Not satisfied with winning the crown, some proud victors have even taken on a more regal ring name.

The ECW Championship was active from August 1994 to April 2001, then again from June 2006 to February 2010.

## 🏆 TITLE TRIVIA

Championships are often retired by holding Unification Matches. The winner carries on the lineage of one championship while the other is discontinued.

WOW!

**221**

Different Hardcore Championship reigns in the Title's brief, four-year history— more than any other title by far.

## Q: WHICH WAS THE FIRST WORLD CHAMPIONSHIP TO BE EXCLUSIVE TO *RAW*?

**A:** The World Heavyweight Championship. Now retired, the classic gold Title was first awarded to Triple H on September 2, 2002. The Title was the property of *RAW* until 2005, when the reigning champion, Batista, was drafted to *SmackDown*.

## ★ BEST-EVER...

### BIZARRE RETIRED TITLE CHANGES

★ **Terri Runnels**
This non-competitor became the fourth female Hardcore Champion when she pinned an already flattened and dazed Stevie Richards during an interview.

★ **Mark Henry**
Jeff Jarrett simply gave Henry the European Title as reward for helping him defeat D-Lo Brown at *SummerSlam 1999*.

★ **Dolph Ziggler**
Although *SmackDown* General Manager Vickie Guerrero had banned the Spear finishing move, Edge used it to defeat Vickie's boyfriend, Dolph Ziggler. Vickie retaliated by overstepping her power and awarding Edge's World Heavyweight Championship to Ziggler.

★ **Mideon**
This eccentric Superstar spotted the European Championship in Shane McMahon's bag and wanted it. Shane handed it over just to get Mideon away from him!

★ **Gerald Briscoe**
Gerald Briscoe took advantage of the unique 24/7 rule that left the Hardcore Championship up for grabs at all times. Briscoe found reigning champion Crash Holly snoozing backstage and placed a hand on Holly's chest while an official whispered the winning three-count.

## FINAL SHOWDOWNS

Superstars etch their names in history when they become the final champion to hold a title prior to its retirement.

### DIVAS CHAMPIONSHIP
CHARLOTTE FLAIR DEFEATED NATALYA AT *ROADBLOCK 2016*.

### WWE WOMEN'S TAG TEAM CHAMPIONSHIPS
THE GLAMOUR GIRLS DEFEATED THE JUMPING BOMB ANGELS IN 1988.

### ECW CHAMPIONSHIP
EZEKIEL JACKSON BECAME THE FINAL ECW CHAMPION IN 2010.

# RETIRED CHAMPIONSHIPS

**MUCH LIKE THE SUPERSTARS** who strive for them, championships come and go but they are forever cherished. The history of sports entertainment is chock-full of epic rivalries and jaw-dropping encounters over titles that are now just a fond memory.

A dream confrontation becomes reality when the legendary D-Generation X and New World Order face off at *WrestleMania 31.*

# FACTIONS, STABLES, & TAG TEAMS

## 04

## TAG TEAM CHAMPIONSHIP, *SUMMERSLAM 2015* (AUGUST 23, 2015)

The New Day looked to regain the Tag Team Championship against the team that ended their first reign—the Prime Time Players—but their path to victory wouldn't be easy. The Lucha Dragons and Los Matadors were also part of the Fatal 4-Way Match. Kofi Kingston managed to pin Fernando of Los Matadors to win the titles for The New Day, beginning a record-breaking championship reign.

**WOW!**

# 483

The number of days of The New Day's second Tag Team Championship reign, the longest in WWE history.

## "THE POWER OF POSITIVITY!"
THE NEW DAY

# THE NEW DAY

**FOR THE LAST** few years, the WWE Universe has been delighted by the endearing antics of The New Day. The trio (and their trombone Francesca) are a vibrant addition to sports entertainment. And they have proven to be just as talented in the ring as they are entertaining out of it.

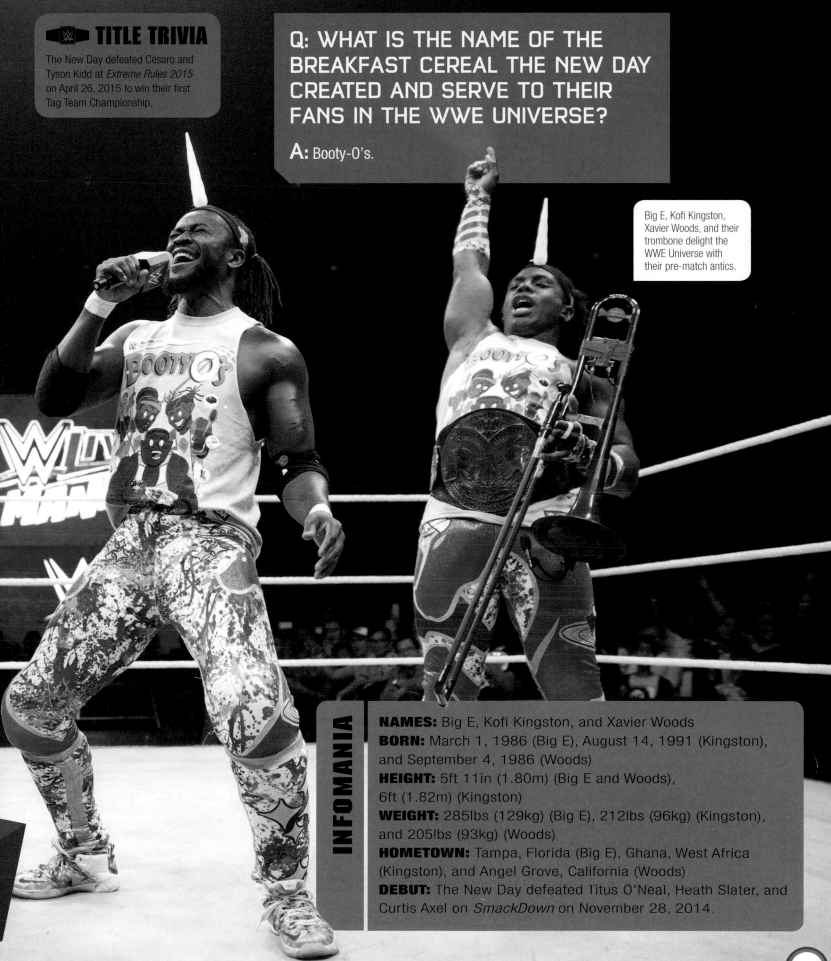

**Q: WHAT IS THE NAME OF THE BREAKFAST CEREAL THE NEW DAY CREATED AND SERVE TO THEIR FANS IN THE WWE UNIVERSE?**

**A:** Booty-O's.

Big E, Kofi Kingston, Xavier Woods, and their trombone delight the WWE Universe with their pre-match antics.

## INFOMANIA

**NAMES:** Big E, Kofi Kingston, and Xavier Woods

**BORN:** March 1, 1986 (Big E), August 14, 1991 (Kingston), and September 4, 1986 (Woods)

**HEIGHT:** 5ft 11in (1.80m) (Big E and Woods), 6ft (1.82m) (Kingston)

**WEIGHT:** 285lbs (129kg) (Big E), 212lbs (96kg) (Kingston), and 205lbs (93kg) (Woods)

**HOMETOWN:** Tampa, Florida (Big E), Ghana, West Africa (Kingston), and Angel Grove, California (Woods)

**DEBUT:** The New Day defeated Titus O'Neal, Heath Slater, and Curtis Axel on *SmackDown* on November 28, 2014.

Triple H assumes leadership of DX alongside Chyna and new members X-Pac and the New Age Outlaws in 1998.

## ★ BEST-EVER...

### DX ACTION

★ **Unforgiven 2006 vs. The McMahons & Big Show**
Vince and Shane McMahon recruited Big Show to help fight their anti-DX cause. Despite a numbers disadvantage, Triple H and Michaels defeated the trio and shoved Vince's head into Big Show's bare behind.

★ **SummerSlam 1998, Triple H vs. The Rock**
For much of 1998, D-Generation X was engaged in warfare with another faction, the Nation of Domination, which featured popular Superstar The Rock. In a fiercely fought *SummerSlam* Ladder Match, DX member Triple H scaled higher than The Rock to grab the Intercontinental Championship.

★ **SummerSlam 2009 vs. Legacy**
DX returned to WWE for what was touted as "one last stand." Triple H and Michaels rode a tank to the ring and proceeded to defeat The Legacy faction, proving they were still WWE's most dominant group.

★ **WrestleMania 31 vs. Sting & nWo**
D-Generation X reunited to interfere on Triple H's behalf while he was locked in a battle with Sting. The group then fended off a counter-attack from the nWo faction!

## WOW! 59

The collective number of championships won by DX members while they competed in WWE.

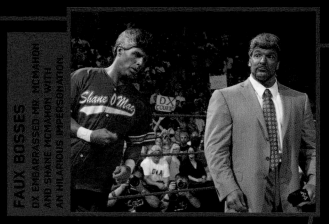
## ANTI-AUTHORITY PRANKS

Throughout the years, D-Generation X found innovative ways to make life miserable for the powers that be. In 2006, their pranking became so unbearable that it drove Mr. McMahon to a nervous breakdown!

### TITLE TRIVIA

Despite their alliance as part of DX, Triple H and Shawn Michaels rarely competed as a tag team. That changed in 2009 when the duo captured the World Tag Team Titles, upending Jeri-Show at *WWE TLC*.

# D-GENERATION X

**FOUNDED IN 1997**, during WWE's "Attitude Era," the faction D-Generation X took adolescent humor from the locker room out into the ring. The more DX noticed that their anti-establishment high jinks irked WWE upper management, the more chaos they caused!

**INFOMANIA**

**DATE OF BIRTH:** August 22, 1985
**HEIGHT:** 6ft 2in (1.87m) (Jey) and 6ft 3in (1.90m) (Jimmy)
**WEIGHT:** 228lbs (103kg) (Jey) and 251lbs (114kg) (Jimmy)
**HOMETOWN:** San Francisco, California
**DEBUT:** The Usos defeated Goldust and Mark Henry on WWE *Superstars* on June 17, 2010.

**Q: THE USOS SUPPORTED JOHN CENA FOR HIS LAST MAN STANDING MATCH AGAINST WHICH SUPERSTAR AT *PAYBACK 2014*?**

**A:** Bray Wyatt.

The Uso brothers keep their opponents reeling by constantly hitting them with devastating double-team moves.

# JEY USO AND JIMMY USO
## THE USOS

**TWIN BROTHERS** The Usos continue the long line of championship-winning WWE tag teams of Samoan ancestry, following in the footsteps of the Wild Samoans and the Headshrinkers. The duo have won multiple tag team championships and they always provide thrilling in-ring action.

## LEADERBOARD

Number of days holding the *RAW* Tag Team Championship.

| NAME | DAYS |
|---|---|
| The New Day | 532 |
| Paul London & Brian Kendrick | 331 |
| MNM | 291 |
| Carlito and Primo Colo | 280 |
| The Usos (Jey and Jimmy) | 257 |
| Miz & Morrison | 250 |
| Kane & Daniel Bryan | 245 |
| The World's Greatest Tag Team | 180 |

## 🏆 TROPHY TRIVIA

The Usos won the Slammy Award for Tag Team of the Year in 2014 and 2015.

## IN DETAIL

### THE USOS VS. THE NEW AGE OUTLAWS, *RAW* (MARCH 3, 2014)

The Usos were finally able to capture their first Tag Team Championship when they ended the sixth title reign of the New Age Outlaws. The brothers held the title for more than six months.

## ★ BEST-EVER...

### USO PAY-PER-VIEW MATCHES

★ *Fatal 4-Way 2010* vs. The Hart Dynasty
Although they came up short in the match, the Usos and Tamina gave a hint of their future championship glory with exciting and high-energy tag team maneuvers in their 2010 pay-per-view debut.

★ *Battleground 2014* vs. The Wyatt Family
The Wyatt Family captured the first fall in a 2 out of 3 Falls Match, forcing the Usos to win two consecutive falls in order to win the match and retain their tag team titles.

★ *Royal Rumble 2015* vs. The Miz and Mizdow
The duo successfully defended their WWE Tag Team Championship title against The Miz and his protégé Mizdow.

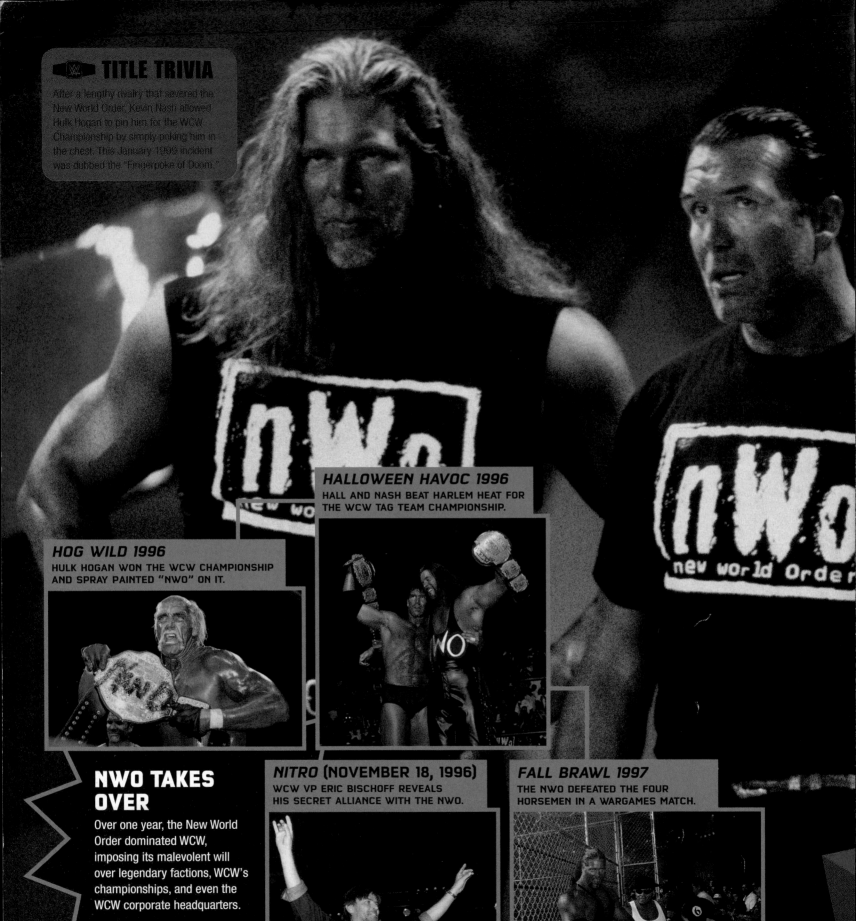

## HALLOWEEN HAVOC 1996

HALL AND NASH BEAT HARLEM HEAT FOR THE WCW TAG TEAM CHAMPIONSHIP.

## HOG WILD 1996

HULK HOGAN WON THE WCW CHAMPIONSHIP AND SPRAY PAINTED "NWO" ON IT.

## NWO TAKES OVER

Over one year, the New World Order dominated WCW, imposing its malevolent will over legendary factions, WCW's championships, and even the WCW corporate headquarters.

## NITRO (NOVEMBER 18, 1996)

WCW VP ERIC BISCHOFF REVEALS HIS SECRET ALLIANCE WITH THE NWO.

## FALL BRAWL 1997

THE NWO DEFEATED THE FOUR HORSEMEN IN A WARGAMES MATCH.

# 62

The number of Superstars and entertainment personalities that were part of The New World Order from 1996 until WCW ended in 2001.

The nWo faction returns to WWE in 2002, looking to recreate the chaos they brought to WCW in 1996.

"YOU WANT A WAR? YOU'RE GONNA GET ONE."

## IN DETAIL

### THE OUTSIDERS VS. TEAM WCW, *BASH AT THE BEACH* (JULY 7, 1996)

Outsiders Scott Hall and Kevin Nash entered their Six-Man Tag Team Match against Team WCW with a disadvantage. Despite weeks of speculation, the rumored third man in their trio was absent. Still, after WCW member Lex Luger left the ring injured, The Outsiders gained the upper hand. Hulk Hogan emerged, seemingly to help WCW. Instead, he shocked fans by hitting Randy Savage with a leg drop, revealing his unthinkable alliance.

# THE NEW WORLD ORDER

**SPORTS ENTERTAINMENT WAS** rocked to its core when WWE Superstars Scott Hall and Kevin Nash invaded WCW, promising to seize control of the brand. The two outsiders struck the first devastating blow when they revealed longtime Superstar Hulk Hogan as the third member of their new insurgent faction.

# 36

Combined number of World Championships that members of The Four Horsemen have won during their careers.

## THE GREAT AMERICAN BASH (JULY 4, 1987)

DUSTY RHODES, NIKITA KOLOFF, THE ROAD WARRIORS, AND PAUL ELLERING DEFEATED RIC FLAIR, ARN ANDERSON, TULLY BLANCHARD, LEX LUGER, AND JJ DILLON.

## WARGAMES

The Four Horsemen competed in more than a dozen WarGames Matches. Their opponents were able to match the Horsemen's numbers by having 4-on-4 or 5-on-5 battles. These matches were also enclosed in a specially designed double cage.

In 2012, the second incarnation of the Four Horsemen with Arn Anderson, Tully Blanchard, manager JJ Dillion, Barry Windham, and Ric Flair was inducted into the WWE Hall of Fame.

## WRESTLEWAR (FEBRUARY 24, 1991)

RIC FLAIR, BARRY WINDHAM, SID VICIOUS, AND LARRY ZBYSZKO DEFEATED STING, BRIAN PILLMAN, AND THE STEINER BROTHERS.

## FALL BRAWL (SEPTEMBER 14, 1997)

THE NWO BEAT RIC FLAIR, STEVE MCMICHAEL, CHRIS BENOIT, AND CURT HENNIG.

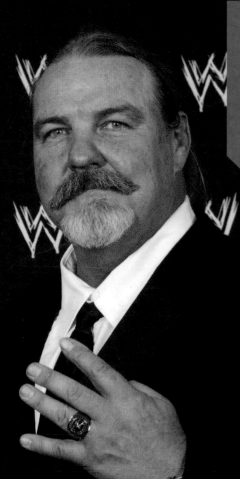

"STING! YOU NEVER WERE A HORSEMAN!"

RIC FLAIR, AFTER THE HORSEMEN TURNED ON FELLOW MEMBER STING

## IN DETAIL

### THE FOUR HORSEWOMEN, *NXT TAKEOVER: BROOKLYN* (AUGUST 22, 2015)

Ric Flair's daughter Charlotte brought a new spin on her father's famous faction by forming an alliance with three other female NXT Superstars: Sasha Banks, Becky Lynch, and Bayley. The quartet promised to revolutionize women's sports entertainment.

# THE FOUR HORSEMEN

NO FACTION IN WCW history was more successful in the ring— and infamous out of the ring—than The Four Horsemen. The team was comprised of various Superstars over the years, but it was always led by the celebrated Superstar Ric Flair.

## HEATWAVE (JULY 18, 1999)

"BROTHER" SPIKE DUDLEY WAS PUT THROUGH TWO FLAMING TABLES.

## SMACKDOWN (MAY 25, 2001)

CHRISTIAN FELT THE BRUNT OF A 3D MOVE FROM THE TOP OF A LADDER.

## GET THE TABLES!

When Bubba Ray had that crazed look in his eyes, the WWE Universe knew what was next. Spectators loved it when Bubba shouted for his partner, D-Von, to fetch some fresh lumber from beneath the ring. Their opponents—not so much.

The Dudleys perform a devastating 3D move on their rival Christian during an episode of *RAW*.

## SMACKDOWN (FEBRUARY 1, 2001)

BUBBA RAY PLANTED JEFF HARDY THROUGH THE WOOD FROM ATOP THE STAGE.

## SMACKDOWN (MAY 11, 2000)

WEIGHING 480LBS (218KG), BIG SHOW WAS VICTIM TO THE WORLD'S HEAVIEST 3D.

## RAW (AUGUST 24, 2015)

AFTER A TEN-YEAR ABSENCE, THE DUDLEYS RETURNED TO WWE AND IMMEDIATELY PUT XAVIER WOODS THROUGH THE TIMBER.

## INFOMANIA

**DATE OF BIRTH:** July 14, 1971 (Bubba Ray) and August 1, 1972 (D-Von)

**HEIGHT:** 6ft 2in (1.88m) (D-Von) and 6ft 3in (1.90m) (Bubba Ray)

**WEIGHT:** 290lbs (132kg) (D-Von) and 280lbs (127kg) (Bubba Ray)

**HOMETOWN:** Dudleyville

**SIGNATURE MOVE:** 3D, short for "Dudley Death Drop"—D-Von lifts an opponent in the air so Bubba Ray can yank him down with force, often through a table.

**DEBUT:** The Dudley Boyz jumped from ECW to WWE in September 1999. They defeated the Hardy Boyz in their first match on *RAW*.

**TITLE TRIVIA**

At *No Way Out 2000*, the Dudley Boyz won their first World Tag Team Championship in WWE by defeating the New Age Outlaws.

## ★ BEST-EVER...

### ► CHAMPIONSHIP TRIUMPHS

★ **Hostile City Showdown 1997**
Shortly after coming together as a villainous duo, Bubba Ray and D-Von defeated The Eliminators (Perry Saturn and John Kronus) to capture their first ECW Tag Team Championships.

★ **SmackDown (October 26, 2001)**
The Dudley Boyz defeated the Hardy Boyz for the WCW Tag Team Championship. With this victory, the duo became the first tag team ever to hold the WWE, ECW, and WCW Tag Team Championships.

★ **SmackDown (June 17, 2004)**
After competing on *RAW* in 2003, Bubba Ray and D-Von were traded to *SmackDown* in March 2004. In June of that year, they beat Charlie Haas and Rico to claim the WWE Tag Team Titles. This made the Dudleys the first team to hold tag team titles on both brands.

**WOW!**

# 24

Combined number of tag team titles the Dudley Boyz have held during their time in sports entertainment.

# BUBBA RAY AND D-VON DUDLEY
## — THE DUDLEY BOYZ —

**THE INFAMOUS DUDLEY BOYZ** have amassed more championships than any tag team in history in over 20 years of competing together. Clad in camouflage, they dominated ECW in the 1990s, then took their rough-and-tumble style to WWE.

"WE SNACK ON DANGER, AND WE DINE ON DEATH!"

THE ROAD WARRIORS

Q: THE ROAD WARRIORS FACED WHICH OTHER LEGENDARY TAG TEAM IN A SCAFFOLD MATCH AT *STARRCADE 1986*?

A: The Midnight Express.

With their spiked shoulder pads and face paint, The Legion of Doom intimidated opponents before they even reached the ring.

# THE LEGION OF DOOM

"OOOHHH, WHAT A RUSH!" When fans heard that phrase, they knew that the most dominant tag team in sports entertainment was headed to the ring. The duo of Hawk and Animal traveled the world, first as The Road Warriors and later as The Legion of Doom, leaving a trail of devastated opponents behind them.

116

## RESULTS TABLE

The Road Warriors are the only team in history to have won the World Tag Team Championship in AWA, WCW, and WWE.

| CHAMPIONSHIP | TEAM THEY DEFEATED | DATE | EVENT |
|---|---|---|---|
| AWA | The Crusher & Baron Von Raschke | August 25, 1984 | Live event |
| WCW | The Midnight Express | October 29, 1988 | Live event |
| WWE | The Nasty Boys | August 26, 1991 | SummerSlam |
| WWE | The Godwinns | October 13, 1997 | RAW |

## 🏆 TROPHY TRIVIA

In 2011, Hawk, Animal, and Paul Ellering were inducted into the WWE Hall of Fame as The Road Warriors.

## IN DETAIL

### IRON TEAM TOURNAMENT, STARRCADE (DECEMBER 13, 1989)

In order to decide who was the greatest tag team of all—or the "Iron Team"—four of the most talented squads met in a round-robin tournament at Starrcade 1989. While they fell to the Steiner Brothers, The Road Warriors claimed decisive victories over Doom and The New Wild Samoans to claim the Iron Team Title.

## WOW! 1

The Road Warriors outlasted 24 tag teams to come first in the first-ever Jim Crockett Sr. Memorial Tag Team Tournament on April 19, 1986 and claim its $1 million prize.

## INFOMANIA

**DATE OF BIRTH:** January 26, 1958 (Hawk) and September 12, 1960 (Animal)

**HEIGHT:** 6ft 3in (1.90m) (Hawk) and 6ft 2in (1.88m) (Animal)

**WEIGHT:** 270lbs (132kg) (Hawk) and 305lbs (138kg) (Animal)

**HOMETOWN:** Chicago, Illinois

**DEBUT:** Defeated Al Burke and Bob Bradley on WWE Wrestling Challenge on July 15, 1990.

## INFOMANIA

**HEIGHT:** 6ft 5in (1.96m) (Edge) and 6ft 1in (1.85m) (Christian)
**WEIGHT:** 241lbs (109kg) (Edge) and 212lbs (96kg) (Christian)
**HOMETOWN:** Toronto, Canada
**SIGNATURE MOVE:** Con-Chair-To—Edge and Christian sandwich a foe between two swinging chairs.
**DEBUT:** First competing as individuals, Edge and Christian came together as members of The Brood in 1998. Along with leader Gangrel, they battled the New Age Outlaws and X-Pac which ended in a No Contest on *RAW* on November 2, 1998.

## ★ BEST-EVER...

### ▶ AWESOME ENCOUNTERS

★ *SummerSlam 2000* vs. The Hardy Boyz vs. The Dudley Boyz
Edge and Christian sent Bubba Ray Dudley flying through four double-stacked tables on their way to winning the first-ever Tables, Ladders, and Chairs Match.

★ *Armageddon 2000*, Four Corners Match
Facing three other top teams including the reigning champions, the Right to Censor, Edge and Christian emerged victorious. Edge's Spear move to Bubba Ray Dudley cleared the way for Christian to score the pin.

★ *WrestleMania X-7* vs. The Hardy Boyz vs. The Dudley Boyz
Proving their first TLC Match was no fluke, Edge and Christian repeated their success. Edge hit Jeff Hardy with a Spear off the top of a ladder in this historic clash, which led to them being Tag Team Champions.

Edge and Christian put their totally awesome teamwork on display by spinning Hardcore Holly through the air with a Double Arm Drag at *SmackDown* in April 2000.

# EDGE AND CHRISTIAN

**EDGE AND CHRISTIAN'S** influence led to the creation of the Tables, Ladders, and Chairs Match. The charismatic duo dominated these new contests on their way to becoming one of WWE's most successful tag teams, backing up their boast that they "totally reeked of awesomeness."

## Q: WHICH TWO SUPERSTARS BECAME TEAMMATES OF EDGE AND CHRISTIAN IN 2001?

**A:** Kurt Angle and Rhyno. With these two allies by their side, Edge and Christian became an even more formidable unit. Angle was a former Olympic gold medalist and WWE Champion. Rhyno was a former ECW standout who possessed the punishing Gore maneuver—similar to Edge's Spear.

## WOW!

# 1

Number of years it took Edge and Christian to collect all seven of their World Tag Team Championships.

## IN NUMBERS ● ● ●

**10** ❯ Wins in pay-per-view matches

**7** ❯ World Tag Team Championships

**3** ❯ TLC/Ladder Match wins

**3** ❯ Combined singles championships held while together as a tag team

### TITLE TRIVIA

Both Edge and Christian would go on to become World Champions. Edge took home this honor a staggering 11 times, while Christian finally claimed his lone World Championship at *Extreme Rules 2011*.

# "FOR THE BENEFIT OF THOSE WITH FLASH PHOTOGRAPHY!"

EDGE AND CHRISTIAN

## FIRST MEMBERS OF THE WWE HEENAN FAMILY

After joining WWE in 1984, Bobby Heenan's first incarnation of the Heenan Family included Paul Orndorff, Ken Patera, King Kong Bundy, and Big John Studd.

## SIZE CHART

| PAUL ORNDORFF | KEN PATERA | KING KONG BUNDY | BIG JOHN STUDD |
|---|---|---|---|
| 6ft (1.83m) | 6ft 2in (1.88m) | 6ft 4in (1.93m) | 6ft 10in (2.08m) |

In addition to his managerial prowess and quick wit, Bobby "The Brain" Heenan was also known for his ostentatious outfits.

## 🏆 TROPHY TRIVIA

In 2004, Bobby "The Brain" Heenan was inducted into the WWE Hall of Fame. He was also joined by Heenan Family members in the Hall of Fame in 2005 and 2007.

## WOW!

# 13

Number of competitors Bobby Heenan managed during his career who would go on to become WWE Hall of Famers.

# THE HEENAN FAMILY

**PERHAPS THE MOST** successful manager in WWE history, Bobby "The Brain" Heenan constantly had a number of villainous clients that he would collectively call the Heenan Family. Whether in the AWA, NWA, or WWE, the Heenan Family was both a championship threat and a constant thorn in the side of good guys everywhere.

**NAME:** Bobby "The Brain" Heenan
**DATE OF BIRTH:** November 1, 1944
**HEIGHT:** 6ft (1.83m)
**WEIGHT:** 190lbs (86kg)
**HOMETOWN:** Beverly Hills, California
**DEBUT:** Managed Big John Studd to a countout victory over WWE Champion Hulk Hogan on September 22, 1984 at Madison Square Garden.

## "A FRIEND IN NEED IS A PEST!"

BOBBY "THE BRAIN" HEENAN

**Q: WHICH SUPERSTAR DID BOBBY HEENAN GUIDE TO THE AWA WORLD HEAVYWEIGHT CHAMPIONSHIP FOUR TIMES?**

**A:** Nick Bockwinkel.

# RESULTS TABLE

WWE championships won by members of the Heenan Family and when they won them.

| HEENAN FAMILY MEMBER | TITLE | DATE | PREVIOUS TITLEHOLDER |
|---|---|---|---|
| ANDRÉ THE GIANT | WWE Championship | February 5, 1988 | Hulk Hogan |
| RICK RUDE | Intercontinental Championship | April 2, 1989 | Ultimate Warrior |
| THE BRAIN BUSTERS | World Tag Team Championship | July 29, 1989 | Demolition |
| THE COLOSSAL CONNECTION | World Tag Team Championship | December 13, 1989 | Demolition |
| MR. PERFECT | Intercontinental Championship | April 23, 1990 | Title was vacated |
| MR. PERFECT | Intercontinental Championship | December 15, 1990 | Texas Tornado |
| RIC FLAIR | WWE Championship | January 19, 1992 | Title was vacated |
| RIC FLAIR | WWE Championship | September 14, 1992 | Randy Savage |

**NAME:** Luke Gallows and Karl Anderson
**HEIGHT:** 6ft 8in (2.03m) (Gallows) and 6ft ½in (1.84m) (Anderson)
**WEIGHT:** 290lbs (130kg) (Gallows) and 215lbs (98kg) Anderson
**HOMETOWN:** Cumberland, Maryland (Gallows) and Asheville, North Carolina (Anderson)
**SIGNATURE MOVE:** Magic Killer— a double-team finisher in which Gallows hoists an opponent up by the shoulders, Anderson grabs his legs, and both men slam him to the canvas.
**DEBUT:** After starting off their career in New Japan Pro Wrestling (NJPW), Gallows and Anderson ambushed sibling duo The Usos on *RAW* on April 11, 2016, confirming rumors of their WWE arrival.

Gallows and Anderson compete in a Tornado Tag Team Match at *Extreme Rules 2016*.

Using their cutting brand of fighting talk, Enzo Amore and Big Cass appear at *SummerSlam 2016* in Brooklyn, New York.

# "I GOT THE GIFT OF GAB AND THE GIFT OF JAB."
ENZO AMORE

**Q: WHICH TAG TEAM DID THE GOLDEN TRUTH DEFEAT FOR THEIR FIRST VICTORY?**

**A:** Breezango. After consecutive losses, The Golden Truth got themselves on track at the *Money in the Bank 2016* kick-off. That summer, they established themselves as a formidable team with wins over The Ascension, The Vaudevillains, and The Social Outcasts.

**WOW!**

**47**

The combined years in sports entertainment between R-Truth and Goldust, making The Golden Truth WWE's most experienced tandem.

Cousins Primo and Epico from Puerto Rico compete as tag team The Shining Stars.

The Golden Truth is comprised of veteran oddballs Goldust and R-Truth.

**TITLE TRIVIA**

Primo and Epico first teamed up in 2011. They won the WWE Tag Team Championship in January 2012 and held it for three months, successfully defending the titles during the *WrestleMania XXVIII* Pre-Show.

# RAW TAG TEAMS

**IN RAW'S FIERCE** tag team division, a close-knit partnership is vital to success. From seasoned veterans like The Golden Truth to fresh newcomers Enzo and Cass, *RAW* tag teams always have each other's back inside the ring and out.

# ★ BEST-EVER...

## ▷ SMACKDOWN TAG TEAM CHAMPIONSHIP TITLE CHANGES

★ *SmackDown* (April 21, 2005), MNM vs. Eddie Guerrero and Rey Mysterio
Joey Mercury, Johnny Nitro, and Melina (MNM) made an incredible first impression, capturing the Tag Team Championship in their first match in WWE from seasoned veterans Eddie Guerrero and Rey Mysterio.

★ *SmackDown* (September 9, 1999), Big Show and Undertaker vs. The Rock 'n' Sock Connection
Perhaps the most effective pairing in the history of WWE, the Unholy Alliance, consisting of Big Show and Undertaker, defeated Mankind and The Rock in a Buried Alive Match to capture the Tag Team Championship for a second time.

★ *SmackDown* (July 4, 2002), Edge and Hulk Hogan vs. Billy and Chuck
Edge managed to capture a Tag Team Championship for the eighth time in his career by teaming with childhood hero Hulk Hogan on a special Independence Day episode of *SmackDown*.

Q: WHICH TAG TEAM DID HEATH SLATER AND RHYNO DEFEAT IN THE FIRST ROUND OF THE TOURNAMENT TO BE CROWNED THE FIRST *SMACKDOWN* TAG TEAM CHAMPIONS?

A: The Headbangers.

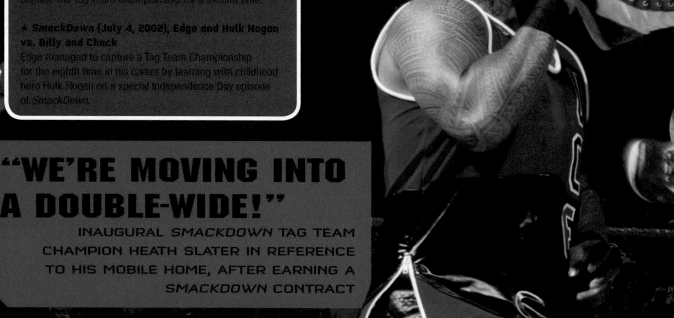

## "WE'RE MOVING INTO A DOUBLE-WIDE!"

INAUGURAL *SMACKDOWN* TAG TEAM CHAMPION HEATH SLATER IN REFERENCE TO HIS MOBILE HOME, AFTER EARNING A *SMACKDOWN* CONTRACT

# SMACKDOWN TAG TEAMS

**WITH THE 2016** brand split between *SmackDown* and *RAW*, new opportunities were developed for WWE Superstars. *SmackDown* saw the creation of a new tag team championship, and numerous pairings—both longstanding and newly created—arose to claim the title.

American Alpha teammates Chad Gable and Jason Jordan nail one of the Usos with a powerful Double Drop Kick.

**TAG TEAM REIGN #1:**
REY MYSTERIO AND EDGE DEFEATED KURT ANGLE AND CHRIS BENOIT IN A 2-OUT-OF-3 FALLS MATCH (NOVEMBER 7, 2002).

**TAG TEAM REIGN #2:**
REY MYSTERIO AND ROB VAN DAM DEFEATED KENZO SUZUKI AND RENE DUPREE (DECEMBER 9, 2004).

**TAG TEAM REIGN #3:**
REY MYSTERIO AND EDDIE GUERRERO DEFEATED THE BASHAM BROTHERS AT NO WAY OUT 2005 (FEBRUARY 20, 2005).

**TAG TEAM REIGN #4:**
REY MYSTERIO AND BATISTA DEFEATED MNM (DECEMBER 13, 2005).

# DOUBLE TROUBLE

While part of *SmackDown*, Rey Mysterio won Tag Team Championships with four different partners. Three of his title wins occurred on the show, with a fourth happening on an exclusive *SmackDown* pay-per-view event.

Davey Boy Smith and Dynamite Kid (along with their beloved bulldog mascot Matilda) were the pride of England in the 1980s as The British Bulldogs.

When brothers Booker T and Stevie Ray teamed together as Harlem Heat, the vibrant duo captured the most WCW Tag Team Championships in history.

## 🏆 TITLE TRIVIA

Despite coming up short in several World Tag Team Championship matches, the British Bulldogs finally earned their only title in WWE at *WrestleMania 2* against The Dream Team.

Two of WWE's greatest daredevils, siblings The Hardy Boyz helped revolutionize WWE with their unique moves and high-flying exploits.

## AKA
The Hardys / Team Xtreme (with Lita) / The New Brood

# LEADERBOARD

Most WCW Tag Team Championship reigns.

| TAG TEAM | NUMBER OF REIGNS |
|---|---|
| Harlem Heat | 10 |
| Minnesota Wrecking Crew | 7 |
| Steiner Brothers | 7 |
| The Outsiders | 6 |
| Ricky Steamboat and Jay Youngblood | 5 |
| Rock 'n' Roll Express | 4 |
| Perfect Event | 3 |
| The Briscoe Brothers | 3 |
| The Harris Brothers | 3 |
| The Nasty Boys | 3 |

Dressed in black studded leather and war paint, Demolition pounded opponents into submission with brute force.

## IN NUMBERS ● ● ●

**478 days** ❯ Demolition's longest championship reign—a record at the time

**27 years** ❯ Length of time that the above record stood for

**3** ❯ Demolition's World Tag Team Championship reigns

**2** ❯ World Tag Team Championships won at *WrestleMania*, also a record

# LEGENDARY TAG TEAMS

**SPORTS-ENTERTAINMENT HISTORY** is overflowing with stellar tag teams who helped pave the way for all the action that the WWE Universe enjoys today. Whether real-life brothers or just two Superstars with a common goal, the combined strength of these terrific tandems vaulted them to championship glory.

## SIBLING RIVALRY REBORN, *RAW* (FEBRUARY 22, 2016)

Mr. McMahon decided to publicly honor his daughter Stephanie for her work in The Authority by awarding her the "Vincent J. McMahon Legacy of Excellence" award. But before he could complete the ceremony, his other child Shane McMahon emerged, returning to WWE for the first time in almost a decade. The event would launch a battle for control of WWE between the siblings that resulted in the *RAW/Smackdown Live* brand split that same year.

"IT'S WHAT'S BEST FOR BUSINESS."

TRIPLE H

"The Authority" was originally the name for power couple Stephanie McMahon and Triple H until they formed a stable of Superstars under the name.

# THE AUTHORITY

**FOR SEVERAL YEARS** now, Stephanie McMahon and her husband Triple H have increased their power and influence in WWE. In order to guide and protect the Superstars they believed should represent the WWE as champions, they created the stable known as The Authority.

**Q: WHEN THE MONSTROUS KANE JOINED THE AUTHORITY, WHAT JOB TITLE DID HE RECEIVE?**

**A:** Director of Operations.

## AUTHORITY ENFORCERS

In order to keep their control of WWE Superstars and protect their hand-picked champions, The Authority employed numerous tough enforcers.

### SIZE CHART

**JAMIE NOBLE**
5ft 9in (1.75m)

**BILLY GUNN**
6ft 3in (1.90m)

**KANE**
7ft (2.13m)

## WOW!

# 29

The Authority enforcer Big Show outlasted 29 other Superstars to win the second annual André the Giant Memorial Battle Royal at *WrestleMania 31*.

## BETRAYAL

THINGS LOOKED BLEAK FOR CENA'S TEAM WHEN BIG SHOW JOINED THE AUTHORITY.

## TITLE TRIVIA

The 2016 Royal Rumble Match was for Roman Reigns' WWE Championship. Triple H entered at number 30 and won, becoming both a two-time *Royal Rumble* winner and a nine-time WWE Champion.

### TEAM CENA

JOHN CENA THOUGHT HE HAD ASSEMBLED THE PERFECT TEAM TO END THE AUTHORITY'S REIGN.

### STING VS. TRIPLE H

STING MAKES HIS WWE IN-RING DEBUT AND ATTACKS TRIPLE H.

## TEAM CENA WINS

WITH STING'S HELP, DOLPH ZIGGLER PINS SETH ROLLINS FOR THE WIN.

## TEAM CENA VS. THE AUTHORITY

At *Survivor Series 2014*, John Cena built a team to face The Authority's hand-picked team with the stipulation that if The Authority won, Cena's team would be fired, but if Team Cena won, The Authority would be stripped of its power.

## 🏆 TROPHY TRIVIA

Michael Cole is a four-time Slammy Award winner, with awards including the "And I Quote" Line of the Year and "Oh My" Moment of the Year.

*RAW* commentators Bryon Saxton, Michael Cole, and Corey Graves.

## "WHAT A MANEUVER!"

MICHAEL COLE

## WOW!

## 20

Number of years in WWE that *RAW* commentator Michael Cole celebrated in 2017.

## ★ BEST-EVER...

### ▶ ANNOUNCERS IN ACTION

**★ *RAW* (April 18, 2005), Jim Ross vs. Triple H**
Forced into a match with Triple H, no one gave Jim Ross any chance in this one-sided encounter... until Batista showed up. Batista laid out Triple H and placed a fallen Ross over the top of him for the pin, handing Triple H an embarrassing defeat.

**★ *WrestleMania XXVII*, Michael Cole vs. Jerry "The King" Lawler**
Cole had pestered his announcing partner for several months. When Lawler finally got his hands on him, the former AWA Champion made the most of it, whipping Cole from pillar to post. Though Lawler dominated the match, he was disqualified due to Stone Cold Steve Austin's involvement.

**★ *Over the Limit 2011*, Michael Cole vs. Jerry "The King" Lawler**
Lawler exacted revenge on Cole in a Kiss My Foot Match. Because the rules specified that the loser would kiss the winner's feet, The King slathered his toes in Jim Ross's barbeque sauce and stuffed them in Cole's mouth!

**★ *RAW* (December 26, 2011), Booker T vs. Cody Rhodes**
*SmackDown* announcer Booker T was lured back to in-ring action by braggart Cody Rhodes. Booker battled Cody in a series of matches. Though he was unable to take away Cody's Intercontinental Championship, he did notch a win over Cody on *RAW* in Chicago, Illinois.

# 280

Number of days John "Bradshaw" Layfield held the WWE Championship for as a *SmackDown* Superstar.

*SmackDown Live* commentators John "Bradshaw" Layfield, Mauro Ranallo, and David Otunga.

## Q: WHERE DID COMMENTATOR DAVID OTUNGA ATTEND LAW SCHOOL?

**A:** Harvard University. The famed university in Cambridge, Massachusetts is the alma mater of Facebook tycoon Mark Zuckerberg, actress Natalie Portman, and former US President Barack Obama.

## 🏆 TROPHY TRIVIA

*SmackDown Live* correspondent Renee Young won a Slammy Award in 2013 for her work on the *JBL & Cole Show*. Today, she is one of WWE's most insightful personalities and the host of *Talkin' Smack* on WWE Network.

# ANNOUNCING TEAMS

**WWE'S ANNOUNCING TEAMS** provide the soundtrack to the jaw-dropping action seen each week on *RAW* and *SmackDown Live*. Their valuable insights and lively commentary are essential in keeping the WWE Universe informed and entertained.

# 05

# BIG EVENTS

Inside the Los Angeles Memorial
Sports Arena, Randy "Macho Man"
Savage and Ultimate Warrior prepare
to collide in a Retirement Match at
*WrestleMania VII*.

**NETWORKS:** USA Network 1993–2000; 2005–present; TNN/Spike 2000–2005

**EPISODE LENGTH:** January 1993–January 1997: one hour; February 1997–July 2012: two hours; July 2012–present: three hours

**DEBUT:** The first *RAW* episode aired on January 11, 1993, and included matches featuring Yokozuna, Shawn Michaels, the Steiner Brothers, and Undertaker.

## ♛ TROPHY TRIVIA

On December 8, 2008, *RAW* hosted the Slammy Awards for the first time and Chris Jericho closed the night by winning Superstar of the Year.

**Q: WHICH LONGTIME WWE SUPERSTAR WON THE MAIN EVENT MATCH ON THE FIRST EPISODE OF *RAW*?**

**A:** Undertaker.

### SHAQUILLE O'NEAL
THE PROFESSIONAL BASKETBALL PLAYER APPEARED ON JULY 27, 2009.

### NANCY O'DELL AND MARIA MENOUNOS
THE ENTERTAINMENT JOURNALISTS APPEARED ON OCTOBER 12, 2009.

## *RAW* GUEST HOSTS

In 2009 and 2010, WWE decided to shake up *RAW* by bringing in well-known guest hosts from different areas of entertainment to serve as one-night-only authority figures.

### MARK CUBAN
THE BUSINESSMAN APPEARED ON DECEMBER 7, 2009.

### DAVID HASSELHOFF
THE ACTOR APPEARED ON APRIL 12, 2010.

**FOR 25 YEARS**, *RAW* has produced some of the most incredible moments in WWE history. The biggest Superstars appear on the Monday night show, which is viewed around the world by millions of people.

## RESULTS TABLE

A wide variety of championships have been defended on *RAW*. The following table lists the first time different titles changed hands on the show.

| SUPERSTAR | TITLE | DATE | PREVIOUS CHAMPION |
|-----------|-------|------|-------------------|
| MARTY JANNETTY | Intercontinental Championship | May 17, 1993 | Shawn Michaels |
| THE QUEBECERS | World Tag Team Championship | September 12, 1993 | The Steiners |
| ALUNDRA BLAYZE | WWE Women's Championship | April 3, 1995 | Bull Nakano |
| SYCHO SID | WWE Championship | February 17, 1997 | Bret Hart |
| TAJIRI | United States Championship | September 10, 2001 | Chris Kanyon |
| TRIPLE H | World Heavyweight Championship | September 2, 2002 | First holder of Title |
| JILLIAN HALL | Divas Championship | October 12, 2009 | Mickie James |
| SHO-MIZ | WWE Tag Team Championship | February 8, 2010 | D-Generation X |
| SASHA BANKS | RAW Women's Championship | July 25, 2016 | Charlotte Flair |
| KEVIN OWENS | WWE Universal Championship | August 29, 2016 | Title was vacated |

## "WELCOME TO *RAW* IS JERICHO!"

CHRIS JERICHO'S INFAMOUS ANNOUNCMENT ON HIS *RAW* DEBUT

*RAW*'s opening fireworks have revved up the WWE Universe for over 20 years.

WOW!

# 1231

Number of episodes *RAW* has aired up to 2016—more than any other episodic weekly primetime show in television history.

## BIG JOHN STUDD, 1989

STUDD WON THE SECOND *ROYAL RUMBLE* AFTER ENTERING 27TH IN THE LINE UP. IT WAS THE FIRST RUMBLE CONTESTED IN THE 30-SUPERSTAR FORMAT.

## BRET HART, 1994

HART ENTERED IN THE 27TH POSITION BUT SHARED THE VICTORY WITH LEX LUGER AFTER THEY HIT THE FLOOR AT THE SAME TIME.

## LUCKY #27

Superstars select their entry number to the Royal Rumble Match at random, hoping to draw as high a number as possible. While most would consider #30 the ideal number, it has not produced the most winners. Four Superstars have emerged as the victor from the 27th position.

**YOKOZUNA, 1993**
THIS MASSIVE SUPERSTAR ELIMINATED RANDY SAVAGE LAST TO WIN THE MATCH.

## Q: WHO WON THE FIRST ROYAL RUMBLE MATCH IN 1988?

**A:** "Hacksaw" Jim Duggan. The inaugural match was the only one to include just 20 Superstars. Duggan entered in the #13 position and joined a scrum that included eight other future WWE Hall of Famers. The hefty Superstar One Man Gang was eliminated last to etch Duggan's name in history as the first Rumble winner.

**STONE COLD STEVE AUSTIN, 2001**
THE #27 SLOT WAS ALL AUSTIN NEEDED TO WIN HIS RECORD THIRD ROYAL RUMBLE MATCH.

## WOW! 900

Number of entrants who have competed in a Royal Rumble Match. Only 23 Superstars have actually won a Rumble.

**THE ROYAL RUMBLE** is one of WWE's most celebrated traditions. Thirty Superstars enter the ring and the last entrant remaining after 29 others have been tossed over the top rope gets the chance to headline *WrestleMania*.

## IN NUMBERS ● ● ●

**559,122** › Number of WWE Universe members who have attended a *Royal Rumble*

**296** › Minutes and 59 seconds—the longest cumulative time spent in Royal Rumble Matches, set by Chris Jericho in 2017

**62** › Minutes and 12 seconds—the longest time in a single Rumble, set by Rey Mysterio in 2006

Apollo Crews aims a dropkick at The Miz while The New Day fight to avoid elimination in the 2017 Royal Rumble Match.

## ★ BEST-EVER...

### ▷ SHOCKING *ROYAL RUMBLE* ELIMINATIONS

**★ Royal Rumble 2017, Brock Lesnar**
After being soundly defeated by Goldberg at *Survivor Series*, most people expected Lesnar to redeem himself when he saw Goldberg enter the Rumble. Instead, Goldberg embarrassed Lesnar again, hitting him with a Spear move and quickly sending him over the ropes.

**★ Royal Rumble 2002, Undertaker**
No one expected Maven to make waves in his first Royal Rumble Match, having just earned a WWE contract on the first season of TV show *Tough Enough*. Jaws dropped when the rookie expelled Undertaker from the match with a powerful dropkick. An enraged Undertaker later returned and made the rookie regret his decision.

**★ Royal Rumble 2010, Great Khali**
All three women who have entered the Rumble have eliminated at least one male competitor, and none more shrewdly than Beth Phoenix in 2010. Phoenix lured the seven-foot-tall Great Khali to the ropes for a kiss, then pulled the smitten giant over the top to his demise.

**★ Royal Rumble 1999, Stone Cold Steve Austin**
WWE Chairman Mr. McMahon entered himself in a Royal Rumble Match during the height of his rivalry with Stone Cold Steve Austin. The Rock provided a distraction while Mr. McMahon heaved Austin out of the ring and eventually won the match.

**"I AM GOING TO TELL YOU ALL WITH A TEAR IN MY EYE, THIS IS THE GREATEST MOMENT OF MY LIFE!"**

RIC FLAIR AFTER WINNING THE 1992 *ROYAL RUMBLE*.

## WRESTLEMANIA DEBUTS OF LEGENDARY SUPERSTARS

Every Superstar dreams of having their *WrestleMania* moment. For these competitors, the opportunity to perform on this grand stage came later in their careers, after they had become world champions in other organizations.

**EVERY SUPERSTAR** wants to make a name for themselves by showcasing their talents at the biggest event in the WWE calendar: *WrestleMania*. Now a week-long event, the extravaganza attracts members of the WWE Universe worldwide.

**JERRY LAWLER**
BATTLED MICHAEL COLE AT *WRESTLEMANIA XXVII.*

**HARLEY RACE**
FACED JUNKYARD DOG IN A LOSER MUST BOW MATCH AT *WRESTLEMANIA III.*

**RIC FLAIR**
DEFENDED THE WWE CHAMPIONSHIP AGAINST RANDY SAVAGE AT *WRESTLEMANIA VIII.*

**STING**
FACED TRIPLE H AT *WRESTLEMANIA 31.*

SECURITY

**Q: WHICH LEGENDARY SPORTS FIGURE SERVED AS THE SPECIAL GUEST REFEREE FOR THE MAIN EVENT OF THE FIRST *WRESTLEMANIA*?**

**A:** Muhammad Ali.

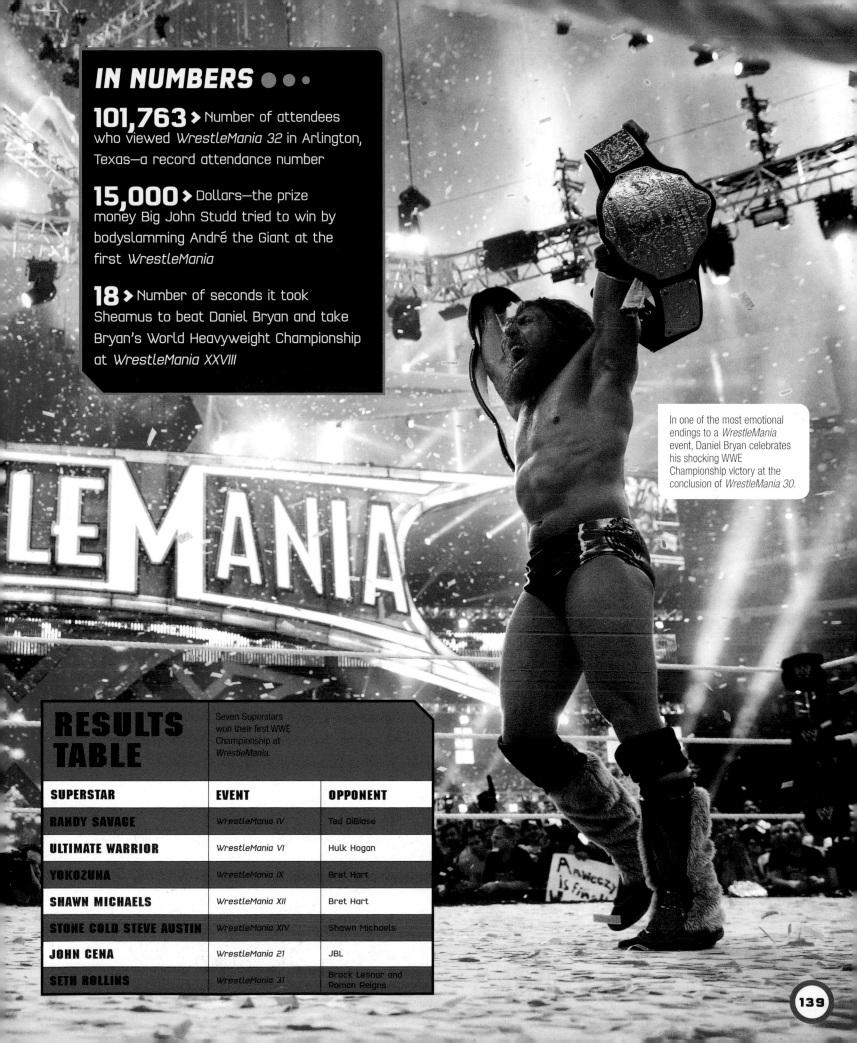

## IN NUMBERS ● ● ●

**101,763** ❯ Number of attendees who viewed *WrestleMania 32* in Arlington, Texas—a record attendance number

**15,000** ❯ Dollars—the prize money Big John Studd tried to win by bodyslamming André the Giant at the first *WrestleMania*

**18** ❯ Number of seconds it took Sheamus to beat Daniel Bryan and take Bryan's World Heavyweight Championship at *WrestleMania XXVIII*

In one of the most emotional endings to a *WrestleMania* event, Daniel Bryan celebrates his shocking WWE Championship victory at the conclusion of *WrestleMania 30*.

## RESULTS TABLE

Seven Superstars won their first WWE Championship at *WrestleMania*.

| SUPERSTAR | EVENT | OPPONENT |
|-----------|-------|----------|
| RANDY SAVAGE | *WrestleMania IV* | Ted DiBiase |
| ULTIMATE WARRIOR | *WrestleMania VI* | Hulk Hogan |
| YOKOZUNA | *WrestleMania IX* | Bret Hart |
| SHAWN MICHAELS | *WrestleMania XII* | Bret Hart |
| STONE COLD STEVE AUSTIN | *WrestleMania XIV* | Shawn Michaels |
| JOHN CENA | *WrestleMania 21* | JBL |
| SETH ROLLINS | *WrestleMania 31* | Brock Lesnar and Roman Reigns |

**WWE SUPERSTARS** lay it all on the line to grab the briefcase hanging from the rafters at a *Money in the Bank* Ladder Match. The briefcase contains a contract that guarantees the winner a championship match at a time of their choosing.

## CALLING YOUR SHOT

Most *Money in the Bank* holders choose to cash in their contract at a time when a reigning champion is vulnerable and does not expect it. Some, for better or worse, take a more honorable approach and give some advance warning.

### ROB VAN DAM, ECW ONE NIGHT STAND 2006
VAN DAM CHALLENGED JOHN CENA WEEKS IN ADVANCE AND WON.

### DEAN AMBROSE, MONEY IN THE BANK 2016
AMBROSE CASHED IN HIS BRIEFCASE THE SAME NIGHT HE WON IT AND BECAME WWE CHAMPION.

### MR. KENNEDY, RAW (MAY 7, 2007)
BEFORE CASHING IT IN, KENNEDY PUT HIS BRIEFCASE ON THE LINE IN A MATCH WITH EDGE AND LOST.

## WOW!

# 2

Number of *Money in the Bank* Ladder Match wins in a row, a feat accomplished by CM Punk (the first two-time winner) at *WrestleMania XXIV* and *WrestleMania 25*.

## WINNERS AND CASH-INS

**WrestleMania 21**
Edge becomes the first-ever *Money in the Bank* winner.

**SmackDown (May 11)**
Edge (who took the *Money in the Bank 2007* briefcase from Mr. Kennedy) defeats Undertaker for the World Heavyweight Title.

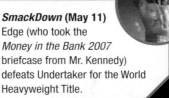

**Extreme Rules**
Having taken *Money in the Bank* for a second time, CM Punk defeats Jeff Hardy for the World Heavyweight Championship.

**2005**    **2006**    **2007**    **2008**    **2009**

# Q: WHO WAS THE FIRST SUPERSTAR TO LOSE THE MATCH IN WHICH HE CASHED IN HIS *MONEY IN THE BANK* CONTRACT?

**A:** Damien Sandow. Before his cash-in match, Sandow used his briefcase to clobber the injured arm of World Heavyweight Champion John Cena. However, Cena found ample strength in his good arm to hoist Sandow into a match-ending Attitude Adjustment move.

The gold version of the *Money in the Bank* briefcase debuted in 2014. Previous versions have been red, blue, and black.

## ★ BEST-EVER...
### SHOCKING CASH-INS

★ *New Years Revolution 2006*, Edge
The first-ever cash-in match laid the blueprint for future winners to follow. John Cena had just won a grueling Elimination Chamber Match and could hardly stand. Edge saw this as the opportune time to challenge the title and took advantage.

★ *Money in the Bank 2010*, Kane
Kane became the first Superstar to win a briefcase and cash in during the same event. He ambushed Rey Mysterio after his match and delivered a Chokeslam move for the win.

★ *SummerSlam 2013*, Randy Orton
Fan-favorite Daniel Bryan proved he was WWE Championship material by defeating John Cena for the prize, but Triple H had other plans. With confetti raining down, Triple H flattened Bryan with a Pedigree move, allowing Randy Orton to cash in.

★ *WrestleMania 31*, Seth Rollins
Seth Rollins was the first Superstar to cash in during a match, and he did it on the most grandiose stage possible. Rollins turned the main event showdown between Brock Lesnar and Roman Reigns into a Triple Threat Match. He pinned Reigns to win the championship.

**RAW (April 8)**
Dolph Ziggler, winner at *Money in the Bank 2012*, defeats Alberto Del Rio to win the World Heavyweight Championship.

**RAW (December 18)**
After the brands *RAW* and *SmackDown* get separate *Money in the Bank* Ladder Matches in 2010, Alberto Del Rio wins the *RAW* briefcase.

**Money in the Bank**
The first *Money in the Bank* Ladder Matches to be distinguished by championships that the winners will contend for (instead of brands) are held this year.

**Money in the Bank**
Sheamus wins the briefcase in June and later defeats Roman Reigns for his World Heavyweight Title in November.

**2010**   **2011**   **2012**   **2013**   **2014**   **2015**

## IN NUMBERS ● ● ●

**64 >** Superstars have entered the Elimination Chamber

**20 >** Number of Elimination Chamber Matches in sports-entertainment history

**8 >** Chris Jericho's record number of Elimination Chamber appearances

**4 >** Triple H's record number of wins in the Elimination Chamber

**2 >** Elimination Chamber Matches in one night, completed by Edge in 2009

## ★ BEST-EVER...
## TABLES, LADDERS, AND CHAIRS TRIUMPHS

**★ RAW (October 7, 2002), Kane**
Kane was forced to defend the World Tag Team Championships without his partner, The Hurricane, so he took on three top tag teams alone and won. His thunderous Chokeslam to Chris Jericho cleared the way for him to scale the ladder.

**★ TLC (December 19, 2010), Edge**
Edge notched his record fifth victory in a Fatal 4-Way TLC Match, outlasting three other Superstars. This marked Edge's final foray in a TLC Match and his sixth World Heavyweight Championship.

**★ TLC (December 16, 2012), The Shield**
Competing in their first official match in WWE, the troublesome trio known as The Shield defeated WWE Tag Team Champions Team Hell No and Ryback. The Shield showed they were a future force in WWE in this first-ever Six-Man TLC Match.

**★ TLC (December 15, 2013), Randy Orton**
The career-long rivalry between John Cena and Randy Orton reached a crescendo when Orton's WWE Championship and Cena's World Heavyweight Championship were unified in this chaotic showdown. Orton used a handcuff to lock Cena to the ropes. He later used the handcuffs to pull Cena off the ladder and win both titles.

Six Superstars enter the Elimination Chamber. Two begin the match while four are contained in separate pods and released at intervals. Superstars are eliminated by pinfall or submission until one winner remains.

**WOW!**

**2** Miles—the length of chain that surrounds the circular steel ring that forms the Elimination Chamber.

**WWE SUPERSTARS** battle in dangerous Hell in a Cell, TLC, and Elimination Chamber events. In these brutal matches, there is no escape and no relief from sustaining damage that may alter their careers forever.

In a TLC Match, tables, ladders, and chairs are legal match accessories and are encouraged. These dangerous objects surround the ring, setting the stage for perilous falls, callous brutality, and unending highlights.

Hell In a Cell is where WWE's most punishing encounters occur. The 20ft high (6.09m) steel structure is completely enclosed, providing no escape and pushing those inside to their absolute limits.

# LEADERBOARD

Most wins in Hell in a Cell Matches.

| SUPERSTAR | WINS |
|---|---|
| Undertaker | 8 |
| Triple H | 6 |
| Shawn Michaels | 3 |
| Randy Orton | 3 |
| Batista | 2 |
| Brock Lesnar | 2 |
| Roman Reigns | 2 |
| CM Punk | 2 |

## RESULTS TABLE

NWA/WCW World Heavyweight Championship title changes at *Starrcade*.

| DATE | NEW CHAMPION | PREVIOUS CHAMPION |
|------|--------------|-------------------|
| NOVEMBER 24, 1983 | Ric Flair | Harley Race |
| NOVEMBER 26, 1987 | Ric Flair | Ron Garvin |
| DECEMBER 27, 1993 | Ric Flair | Big Van Vader |
| DECEMBER 27, 1995 | Ric Flair | Randy Savage |
| DECEMBER 28, 1997 | Sting | "Hollywood" Hulk Hogan |
| DECEMBER 27, 1998 | Kevin Nash | Goldberg |

## 🏆 TROPHY TRIVIA

*Starrcade 1989* featured Iron Man and Iron Team tournaments, where competitors competed against each other in turn during several matches that night. Sting won the title of Iron Man and the Road Warriors were crowned the Iron Team.

**THE NWA AND WCW** entertained fans for 18 years with the top-billing event of the year, *Starrcade*. The event featured some of the biggest names in sports entertainment, who all joined the show to settle long-standing rivalries.

WCW Superstars compete in the Battle Royal at *Starrcade 1991*.

## IN DETAIL

### BATTLEBOWL: THE LETHAL LOTTERY (DECEMBER 29, 1991)

*Starrcade* was the setting for *BattleBowl: The Lethal Lottery* in 1991 and 1992. Some 40 competitors were randomly assigned partners for a tag team match. The winners were then entered into a final battle royal to determine the *BattleBowl* winner. In 1991, fan-favorite Sting was paired with his rival, the brutal Abdullah the Butcher. Despite being attacked by his own partner, Sting managed to win his tag team match and then the *BattleBowl* battle royal by eliminating Lex Luger.

# NIGHT OF THE SKYWALKERS

*Starrcade 1986* featured the first-ever Scaffold Match. Two teams battled 20ft (7m) above the ring with a goal of tossing their opponents down to the ring below.

## BLIND WARRIOR

MIDNIGHT EXPRESS'S DENNIS CONDREY THROWS POWDER IN ROAD WARRIOR HAWK'S EYES.

## HANGING BY A THREAD

ROAD WARRIOR ANIMAL TRIES TO KICK BOBBY EATON OFF THE SCAFFOLD AS HE DANGLES IN THE AIR.

## CAUTIOUS APPROACH

THE ROAD WARRIORS AND MIDNIGHT EXPRESS ARE CAREFUL AT THE START OF THE MATCH.

## WOW!

# 14

Number of World Heavyweight Championships that were defended at *Starrcade* events over its history.

**Q: RODDY PIPER DEFEATED GREG VALENTINE IN WHICH UNIQUE MATCH TYPE AT THE FIRST *STARRCADE* IN 1983?**

**A:** Dog Collar Match.

**Q: WHO BATTLED UNDERTAKER IN ONE OF THE STRANGEST MATCHES OF ALL TIME IN THE SUMMERSLAM 1994 MAIN EVENT?**

**A:** Undertaker! He took on an imposter version of himself and won.

**AS THE PREMIER** sports-entertainment event of the summer, *SummerSlam* offers the WWE Universe incredible championships. It is also the place to showcase intense rivalries between some of WWE's greatest Superstars.

## ★ BEST-EVER...

### SUMMERSLAM MATCHES WITH AN ODD STIPULATION

★ *SummerSlam 2005*, **Rey Mysterio vs. Eddie Guerrero**
Eddie claimed to be the real father of Rey's son, Dominick. To settle matters, they agreed to have a Ladder Match for the custody of Dominick, which Rey won.

★ *SummerSlam 1992*, **Shawn Michaels vs. Rick Martel**
Sensational Sherri managed both men, so when the two decided to fight at *SummerSlam*, she insisted that both agreed to not hit each other in the face in an attempt to preserve the looks of her two clients.

★ *SummerSlam 2008*, **Glamarella (Beth Phoenix and Santino Marella) vs. Kofi Kingston and Mickie James**
In an intergender tag team match, both the Intercontinental and WWE Women's Titles were up for grabs. By pinning James, Phoenix claimed the Women's Championship for herself and the Intercontinental Championship for her partner.

Triple H returns from injury at *SummerSlam 2007* to battle King Booker.

## LEADERBOARD

Superstars with most *SummerSlam* victories.

| SUPERSTAR | NUMBER OF VICTORIES |
|---|---|
| Undertaker | 10 |
| Triple H | 8 |
| Edge | 8 |
| Bret Hart | 7 |
| Hulk Hogan | 6 |
| Shawn Michaels | 6 |
| Kane | 6 |
| Chris Jericho | 6 |
| Randy Orton | 6 |

## "GET READY FOR THE BIGGEST PARTY OF THE SUMMER!"

WWE'S SLOGAN FOR *SUMMERSLAM*

## 2010
TEAM WWE DEFEATED THE NEXUS STABLE IN A 7 ON 7 ELIMINATION MATCH.

## 2009
CM PUNK DEFEATED JEFF HARDY IN A TLC MATCH FOR THE WORLD HEAVYWEIGHT CHAMPIONSHIP.

## WEST COAST ACTION

From 2009 through 2014, Los Angeles served as the permanent home of *SummerSlam*. The six events witnessed some exciting matches.

## 2011
CM PUNK DEFEATED JOHN CENA FOR THE WWE CHAMPIONSHIP. ALBERTO DEL RIO CASHED IN HIS *MONEY IN THE BANK* OPPORTUNITY AND WON THE TITLE.

## 2012
BROCK LESNAR DEFEATED TRIPLE H IN A NO DISQUALIFICATION MATCH.

## 2013
RANDY ORTON CASHED IN HIS *MONEY IN THE BANK* OPPORTUNITY AMD DEFEATED DANIEL BRYAN TO WIN THE WWE CHAMPIONSHIP.

## 2014
BROCK LESNAR DEFEATED JOHN CENA FOR THE WWE CHAMPIONSHIP.

### TITLE TRIVIA

With his victory over Intercontinental Champion The Honky Tonk Man at the inaugural *SummerSlam* on August 29, 1988, the Ultimate Warrior became the first Superstar to win a championship at *SummerSlam*.

## LEGENDS OF *SMACKDOWN*

*SmackDown*'s best competitors have come in big and small packages. Each of these classic Superstars has won a World Championship while serving exclusively under the *SmackDown* brand.

## SIZE CHART

**REY MYSTERIO**
5ft 6in (1.71m)

**EDDIE GUERRERO**
5ft 8in (1.77m)

**KURT ANGLE**
6ft (1.83m)

**THE GREAT KHALI**
7ft 1in (2.15m)

## Q: WHO WAS THE FIRST WOMAN DRAFTED FROM NXT TO *SMACKDOWN LIVE*?

**A:** Alexa Bliss. Bliss was the 47th person to be selected from NXT in the 2016 WWE Draft. Less than five months later, she defeated *SmackDown Live*'s first female pick, Becky Lynch, to become *SmackDown* Women's Champion.

## IN NUMBERS ● ● ●

**280** ❯ Days—the longest WWE Championship reign in *SmackDown* history, held by JBL

**60** ❯ Minutes—the longest one-on-one match in *SmackDown* history, with Kurt Angle against Brock Lesnar

**6** ❯ Number of WWE Hall of Famers who were on the original *SmackDown Live* roster

**1st** ❯ The first pick for *SmackDown Live* in the 2016 WWE Draft was Dean Ambrose

## IN DETAIL

## RHYNO VS. CHRIS JERICHO, *SMACKDOWN* (APRIL 9, 2001)

After a decisive victory over Hugh Morris, Chris Jericho believed he was in for an uneventful night. He was sorely mistaken. Rhyno attacked him as he made his way from the ring toward the curtain and drove Jericho through *SmackDown*'s massive, oval-shaped screen with his signature Gore move. Although the *SmackDown Live* set was destroyed, a new set debuted soon after featuring a giant, metallic fist. The fist would become an iconic symbol of the brand.

# "SMACKDOWN LIVE IS ALL ABOUT BREAKING GLASS CEILINGS..."

SHANE MCMAHON

**WHEN THE ROCK** promised to "lay the *SmackDown*," WWE history was altered forever. *SmackDown Live* was created and named after The Rock's famous quip. The popular show now delivers heart-stopping action every week.

Undertaker's ominous entrance has sent chills down the spines of countless *SmackDown* legends.

## ★ BEST-EVER...

### SMACKDOWN SUPREMACY

**★ Survivor Series 2016, Men's Elimination Match**
The men of *SmackDown Live* reigned supreme when *SmackDown* Superstars were pitted against *RAW* for the first time since the 2016 WWE Draft. Randy Orton sacrificed himself by taking a Roman Reigns Spear maneuver that kept Bray Wyatt free to hit a match-ending Sister Abigail move.

**★ Bragging Rights 2009/2010**
For two years, *SmackDown Live* and *RAW* held a series of matches to prove which brand was superior. At both events, *SmackDown* was victorious and received the *Bragging Rights* Trophy.

**★ Survivor Series 2005, SmackDown vs. RAW Elimination Match**
Tension between WWE's competing brands was sky high in the first-ever *SmackDown* vs. *RAW* Elimination Match. *SmackDown*'s Randy Orton, normally reviled, was a hero to his peers for a brief moment when he hit his winning RKO move on *RAW*'s Shawn Michaels.

**★ WrestleMania XXIV, Battle for Brand Supremacy**
For this inter-promotional showdown, *SmackDown* General Manager Teddy Long selected Batista to combat *RAW's* Umaga, who had been chosen by *RAW* General Manager, William Regal. Batista avoided Umaga's dreaded Samoan Spike move and introduced the monstrous Superstar to his own finisher: the Batista Bomb. The impact left Umaga laying flat on the ground for an easy pin and proved *SmackDown*'s superiority on WWE's grandest stage.

## WOW! 900

Number of *SmackDown Live* episodes celebrated on November 15, 2016. It was marked by the return of the show's most iconic figure: Undertaker.

## EXTREME MOMENTS

Anything goes at *Extreme Rules*. Superstars may go as far as hitting each other with the kitchen sink… literally!

Dean Ambrose and Chris Jericho battle it out surrounded by thumbtacks in the first-ever Asylum Match.

### EXTREME RULES 2009
EDGE AND JEFF HARDY TUMBLED THROUGH A LADDER RESTING ON THE BARRICADE.

### EXTREME RULES 2012
CM PUNK BLASTED CHRIS JERICHO WITH A FIRE EXTINGUISHER.

### EXTREME RULES 2013
RYBACK TACKLED JOHN CENA THROUGH THE STAGE WALL.

### EXTREME RULES 2014
DANIEL BRYAN SENT KANE CRASHING THROUGH A FLAMING TABLE.

### EXTREME RULES 2015
ROMAN REIGNS TRAPPED BIG SHOW UNDER A TABLE TO WIN A LAST MAN STANDING MATCH.

## IN DETAIL

### DEAN AMBROSE VS. CHRIS JERICHO, *EXTREME RULES* (MAY 22, 2016)

In a match only Dean Ambrose's warped mind could concoct, Ambrose and Chris Jericho stepped inside not just any steel cage, but one with a disturbing slew of dangerous objects dangling over their heads! Jericho used several to his advantage during the Asylum Match, such as a kendo stick and a plank of wood wrapped in barbed wire. However, Ambrose reversed Jericho's Codebreaker move and planted him on a bed of thumbtacks to win the match.

**FROM THE BRUTAL** to the downright bizarre, *Extreme Rules* is an event where nothing is off-limits. Typically the first major event after *WrestleMania*, these matches are often a chance for Superstars to do almost anything to settle their scores.

 ## TITLE TRIVIA

In 2016, Charlotte Flair became the first Superstar to defend the WWE Women's Championship in a Submissions Match. Charlotte retained the Title when Natalya tapped out of her signature Figure-Eight Leglock hold.

 ## ★ BEST-EVER...

### ▶ BIZARRE *EXTREME RULES* MATCHES

**★"Kiss My Arse" Match, Dolph Ziggler vs. Sheamus**
Rules stated that the loser must do exactly as the name of the match suggests. However, a defeated Sheamus did not honor the stipulation. Instead, he attacked and rubbed his own behind in Dolph's face!

**★ WeeLC Match, El Torito vs. Hornswoggle**
In this pint-sized version of the TLC Match, WWE's smaller Superstars were armed with miniature tables, ladders, and chairs and left to battle it out in the ring. El Torito put Hornswoggle through a table to win the match.

**★ Strap Match, JTG vs. Shad**
Former Cryme Tyme teammates Shad and JTG were tethered together by a leather strap. The only way to win was to touch all four ring corners. Though JTG was smaller than his opponent, he used a bit of guile to steal a rare victory.

**★ Hog Pen Match, Vickie Guerrero vs. Santina Marella**
Losing stinks, especially when the loser is pinned inside a Hog Pen! Surrounded by live pigs (and the natural products of their digestive tracts), Santina doused both Vickie and her meddling nephew Chavo Guerrero with slop, then pinned Vickie to retain the Miss *WrestleMania* sash.

## "WHEN YOU ENTER MY WORLD, YOU WILL SCREAM, CRY, AND BEG FOR MERCY!"

DEAN AMBROSE

## Q: WHICH CITY HOSTED THE FIRST TWO *SURVIVOR SERIES* EVENTS?

**A:** Richfield, Ohio.

For three decades, the WWE Universe has eagerly anticipated November's *Survivor Series* event, with its incredible matches, amazing debuts, and shocking betrayals.

## RESULTS TABLE

Several of the biggest Superstars in WWE history have won their first-ever WWE Championship at *Survivor Series*.

| SUPERSTAR | DATE | PREVIOUS CHAMPION |
|---|---|---|
| UNDERTAKER | November 27, 1991 | Hulk Hogan |
| SYCHO SID | November 17, 1996 | Shawn Michaels |
| THE ROCK | November 15, 1998 | Title was vacated |
| BIG SHOW | November 14, 1999 | Triple H |
| ROMAN REIGNS | November 22, 2015 | Title was vacated |

### FIRST ROUND
THE ROCK DEFEATED BIG BOSS MAN.

**QUARTERFINALS**
THE ROCK PINNED KEN SHAMROCK.

**SEMIFINALS**
HE WENT ON TO BEAT UNDERTAKER.

## DEADLY GAMES TOURNAMENT

In 1998, *Survivor Series* hosted a 14-man tournament for the vacant WWE Championship. That night, The Rock beat four men to claim his first WWE Championship.

**FINALS**
THE ROCK DEFEATED MANKIND FOR THE WIN.

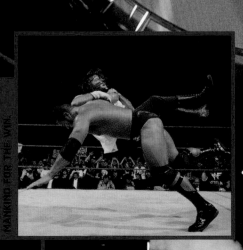

**IN 1987**, WWE expanded its pay-per-view offerings with a new annual event: *Survivor Series*. During the popular show, teams of five Superstars clash in fierce matches until all members of one team have been eliminated.

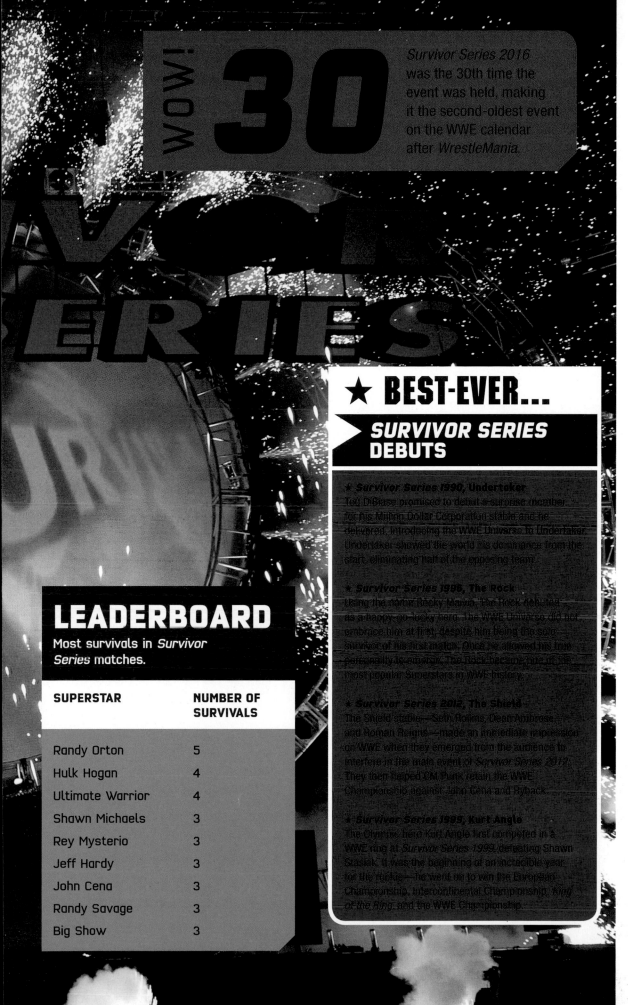

## WOW! 30

*Survivor Series 2016* was the 30th time the event was held, making it the second-oldest event on the WWE calendar after *WrestleMania*.

## ★ BEST-EVER...

### SURVIVOR SERIES DEBUTS

★ **Survivor Series 1990, Undertaker**
Ted DiBiase promised to debut a surprise member for his Million Dollar Corporation stable and he delivered, introducing the WWE Universe to Undertaker. Undertaker showed the world his dominance from the start, eliminating half of the opposing team.

★ **Survivor Series 1996, The Rock**
Using the name Rocky Maivia, The Rock debuted as a happy-go-lucky hero. The WWE Universe did not embrace him at first, despite him being the sole survivor of his first match. Once he allowed his true personality to emerge, The Rock became one of the most popular Superstars in WWE history.

★ **Survivor Series 2012, The Shield**
The Shield stable—Seth Rollins, Dean Ambrose, and Roman Reigns—made an immediate impression on WWE when they emerged from the audience to interfere in the main event of *Survivor Series 2012*. They then helped CM Punk retain the WWE Championship against John Cena and Ryback.

★ **Survivor Series 1999, Kurt Angle**
The Olympic hero Kurt Angle first competed in a WWE ring at *Survivor Series 1999*, defeating Shawn Stasiak. It was the beginning of an incredible year for the rookie—he went on to win the European Championship, Intercontinental Championship, King of the Ring, and the WWE Championship.

## LEADERBOARD

Most survivals in *Survivor Series* matches.

| SUPERSTAR | NUMBER OF SURVIVALS |
| --- | --- |
| Randy Orton | 5 |
| Hulk Hogan | 4 |
| Ultimate Warrior | 4 |
| Shawn Michaels | 3 |
| Rey Mysterio | 3 |
| Jeff Hardy | 3 |
| John Cena | 3 |
| Randy Savage | 3 |
| Big Show | 3 |

## "THIS IS WHERE THE BIG BOYS PLAY, HUH?"

— KEVIN NASH

**ONCE WWE'S CHIEF RIVAL,** WCW is now a celebrated part of its history. From 1995 to 2001, WCW's flagship program, *Monday Nitro*, and *RAW* battled for sports-entertainment superiority.

## ★ BEST-EVER...

### ▶ WCW RIVALRIES

**★ Diamond Dallas Page vs. "Macho Man" Randy Savage**

Page's vendetta with the New World Order put him at odds with Savage, who had joined the insidious faction. When Page's wife Kimberly found herself in the crosshairs, this rivalry turned personal.

**★ Ric Flair vs. Vader**

Vader was a mountain of a Superstar, full of bad intentions—chief among them was ending Ric Flair's career at *Starrcade 1993*. Though Vader received help from another Flair rival, Harley Race, Flair escaped with his career and the WCW Title.

**★ Ric Flair vs. Sting**

Flair recruited longstanding rival Sting into his Four Horsemen stable. When Sting became a threat to Flair's World Title, the Horsemen kicked him out, causing hostility that would last many years.

**★ Dean Malenko vs. Eddie Guerrero**

These agile competitors battled throughout the 1990s. Both men possessed an encyclopedia of submission holds and it showed when they met. Their encounters resembled a full-contact chess match between the ropes.

## Q: WHICH WCW MATCH FEATURED TWO CONNECTED RINGS INSIDE A RECTANGULAR CAGE?

**A:** WarGames. In this notorious match type, two teams of four or more Superstars battled until a member of either team submitted. With no disqualifications, these contests were some of WCW's most brutal. WWE Hall of Famer Dusty Rhodes is credited with inventing WarGames and also participated in several of the matches.

## WOW!

# 84

Number of consecutive weeks that *Monday Nitro* beat *RAW* during the Monday Night War—their battle for ratings.

## WHERE THE BIG BOYS PLAY

WCW touted the strength of their roster with the slogan, "Where the Big Boys Play." While many were big in stature, others packed a king-sized dose of athletic prowess and charisma.

### SIZE CHART

**JUSHIN "THUNDER" LIGER**
5ft 7in (1.70m)

**STING**
6ft 2in (1.88m)

**DIAMOND DALLAS PAGE**
6ft 5in (2m)

**KEVIN NASH**
6ft 10in (2.08m)

WOW!

# 52

Age of Terry Funk during his last ECW Championship reign. The hardcore icon was one of the most influential ECW stars.

Tazz shows why he was nicknamed "The Human Suplex Machine" with this forceful German suplex move on rival Rob Van Dam.

## LEADERBOARD

Most number of days as ECW Champion.

| SUPERSTAR | NUMBER OF DAYS |
|---|---|
| Shane Douglas | 874 |
| The Sandman | 446 |
| Raven | 379 |
| Tazz | 261 |
| Christian | 247 |
| Terry Funk | 208 |
| Mike Awesome | 201 |
| Don Muraco | 174 |
| Justin Credible | 162 |
| Big Show | 152 |
| Lashley | 147 |
| CM Punk | 143 |
| Matt Hardy | 127 |

**E-C-W! E-C-W! E-C-W!** The renegade promotion known as Extreme Championship Wrestling (ECW) helped revolutionize sports entertainment. Its eclectic group of Superstars gave new meaning to hardcore wrestling, attracting throngs of enthusiastic fans.

## AKA

Tazz—"The Human Suplex Machine" /
Shane Douglas—"The Franchise of ECW" /
Super Crazy—"The Insane Luchador" /
Tommy Dreamer—"The Innovator of Violence"

> ## "PROFESSIONAL WRESTLING AS IT WAS MEANT TO BE."
> SHANE DOUGLAS

## ★ BEST-EVER...
### EXTREME ECW MATCHES

★ **Taipei Death Match, Ian Rotten vs. Axel Rotten**
Not for sensitive eyes or the squeamish, this match involved hands dipped in glue and broken glass. Perhaps most disturbing was that the competitors were brothers.

★ **Weapons Match, Tommy Dreamer vs. Brian Lee**
Foreign objects were nothing out of the ordinary in ECW, but this match took it to a different level. Frying pans, a stop sign, mailbox, trashcan, guitar, and baseball bat all made an appearance before Dreamer got the win.

★ **Barbed Wire Match, Terry Funk vs. Sabu**
Ring ropes were removed and replaced with barbed wire. The level of pain each competitor withstood was disturbing even to ECW promoter Paul Heyman, who never scheduled another match like it.

★ **Chicago Street Fight, Dudley Boyz vs. Spike Dudley and Balls Mahoney**
Spike Dudley launched himself off a balcony onto his foes, but it wasn't enough to win this insane tag team match. The Dudleys prevailed after slamming Mahoney through a flaming table covered in thumbtacks.

## TITLE TRIVIA

Soon after ECW's revival in 2006, Big Show defeated Rob Van Dam to become ECW Champion. Longtime ECW fans were furious to see a WWE mainstay claim the title but Big Show didn't care. His victory made him the first Superstar ever to win the WWE, WCW, and ECW Championships.

Spectators and crew members prepare for another night of NXT action inside Full Sail Live, the home of NXT in Orlando, Florida.

# SUPERSTARS OF TOMORROW

## 06

Once the manager of the legendary Road Warriors, Paul Ellering now leads brutal NXT duo The Authors of Pain.

NXT standouts Bobby Roode and Tye Dillinger continue their simmering rivalry at *NXT TakeOver: Toronto* in November 2016.

## "THE FUTURE IS NOW!"

TRIPLE H

## INTERNATIONAL SUPERSTARS

VETERAN STARS LIKE SHINSUKE NAKAMURA AND SAMOA JOE HAVE WORLDWIDE ACCLAIM.

## WOMEN'S WRESTLING

NXT FEATURES STRONG FEMALE SUPERSTARS, SUCH AS EMBER MOON AND ASUKA.

## WHY NXT IS AWESOME

While NXT is the springboard to making it onto *RAW* or *SmackDown Live*, it also stands on its own as a WWE brand. In its brief history, its fan base has grown from cult following to full-blown NXT Universe. These are just some of the reasons why.

**FULL SAIL UNIVERSITY**
THE HOME OF NXT IN FLORIDA HAS A TRULY RAUCOUS ATMOSPHERE.

**STRONG LEADERSHIP**
NXT'S CREATOR, TRIPLE H, OVERSEES AN ALL-STAR COACHING STAFF FULL OF FORMER SUPERSTARS.

## INFOMANIA

**NAME:** Bobby Roode

**DATE OF BIRTH:** May 11, 1977

**HEIGHT:** 6ft (1.83m)

**WEIGHT:** 235lbs (107kg)

**HOMETOWN:** Toronto, Canada

**NICKNAME:** The Glorious One

**SIGNATURE MOVE:** Crossface—a submission hold in which Bobby Roode locks his wrist across an opponent's face.

**DEBUT:** He was spotted in the crowd at *NXT TakeOver: Dallas* in April 2016, and joined NXT soon after.

# NXT: THE FUTURE OF WWE

**SUPERSTARS IN NXT** come from all over the globe, looking to achieve their dreams. These exciting athletes deliver such thrilling action that many believe NXT is on the brink of taking over WWE. Popular NXT Superstars Asuka, Shinsuke Nakamura, and Bobby Roode could make an impact on *RAW* or *SmackDown Live*.

## SUPERSTARS IN TRAINING

From future Superstars to announcers, the Performance Center provides the knowledge and the equipment to put them on a path to success. It is up to the trainees themselves to make the most of their opportunities.

### STRENGTH AND CONDITIONING

SUPERSTARS SCULPT THEIR PHYSIQUES WITH TOP-OF-THE-LINE WEIGHTS AND EQUIPMENT.

### ATHLETICISM

RINGS, ROPES, SANDBAGS, AND OTHER HELPFUL TOOLS HELP SUPERSTARS TRAIN AS ATHLETES.

### THE NEXT VOICE OF WWE

ASPIRING ANNOUNCERS AND COMMENTATORS WORK ON THEIR CRAFT.

### CRASH RING

HIGHFLIERS PRACTICE AERIAL MANEUVERS WITH A SAFE LANDING PAD.

## "THE PERFORMANCE CENTER HAS CHANGED MY WHOLE LIFE."

BAYLEY

## IN NUMBERS ● ● ●

**26,000** ➤ Square feet—the size of the Performance Center

**65** ➤ Approximate number of trainees at any given time

**7** ➤ Training rings

**5** ➤ Levels of training—Beginner, Intermediate 1, Intermediate 2, Advanced, and Polishing

The Green Screen Room is where Superstars develop their characters, using cutting-edge technology to simulate any environment.

Superstars hone their presentation skills in a room dubbed "The Mirror," and even receive direct feedback from WWE Headquarters in Connecticut.

Athletes divide into training groups based on experience and skill level. Each group works with its coach in one of seven rings.

# PERFORMANCE CENTER

**INSIDE WWE'S** state-of-the-art training facility, the Performance Center, future Superstars learn about every aspect of life in WWE, from in-ring skills to perfecting charisma and personality. Students enter as trainees and leave ready to conquer the world of sports entertainment.

## LEADERBOARD

Most matches on NXT specials.

| SUPERSTAR | NUMBER OF MATCHES |
|---|---|
| Finn Bálor | 9 |
| Baron Corbin | 9 |
| Bayley | 8 |
| Samoa Joe | 8 |
| Sami Zayn | 7 |
| Tyler Breeze | 7 |
| The Revival | 7 |
| Asuka | 7 |

### 🏆 TROPHY TRIVIA

The match between Bayley and Sasha Banks at *NXT TakeOver: Brooklyn* in August 2015 was selected as NXT Match of the Year for 2015.

WOW!

## 29

Number of seconds it took Baron Corbin to prove his dominance over CJ Parker at *NXT TakeOver: Fatal 4-Way* on September 11, 2014.

# NXT TAKEOVER SPECIALS

**AFTER MAKING A NAME** for themselves with a loyal audience in NXT's "home" arena—Full Sail University in Winter Park, Florida—the Superstars of NXT are able to show their incredible skills and talent to a worldwide audience thanks to a series of specials on the WWE Network.

# KEVIN OWENS AT *NXT TAKEOVER* EVENTS

WWE Universal Champion Kevin Owens appeared at four NXT *Takeover* specials and his presence changed the course of the NXT Championship.

## NXT TAKEOVER: R EVOLUTION

AFTER BEATING CJ PARKER IN HIS NXT DEBUT, OWENS ATTACKED NEW NXT CHAMPION SAMI ZAYN AT THE END OF THE NIGHT.

## NXT TAKEOVER: RIVAL

KEVIN OWENS DEFEATED SAMI ZAYN VIA TECHNICAL KNOCKOUT TO WIN THE NXT CHAMPIONSHIP.

## NXT TAKEOVER: BROOKLYN

IN A LADDER MATCH AGAINST FINN BÁLOR, KEVIN OWENS WAS DEFEATED.

## NXT TAKEOVER: UNSTOPPABLE

KEVIN OWENS AND SAMI ZAYN'S MATCH ENDED IN A DRAW AND OWENS RETAINED THE NXT CHAMPIONSHIP.

## ★ BEST-EVER...

### NXT TAKEOVER: DEBUTS

★ **NXT TakeOver: R Evolution, Finn Bálor**
After first competing, Finn Bálor went on to team with Hideo Itami to defeat The Ascension. Bálor would go on to win the NXT Championship and WWE Universal Championship.

★ **NXT TakeOver: Brooklyn II, Ember Moon**
In her in-ring debut on August 20, 2016, Ember Moon defeated Billie Kay and seemed poised to be a top challenger for the NXT Women's Championship.

★ **NXT TakeOver: The End, The Authors of Pain**
While not competing in a match, The Authors of Pain made their presence known to the NXT roster by brutally attacking former Tag Team Champions American Alpha after their match.

★ **NXT TakeOver: Brooklyn, Jushin "Thunder" Liger**
One of the most decorated Japanese Superstars in history, Liger had never competed in a WWE ring until August 22, 2015, when he beat Tyler Breeze in the opening match.

# IN NUMBERS ● ● ●

**285** ❯ Pounds (129kg)—the weight of Big E Langston, the heaviest NXT Champion of all time

**194** ❯ Pounds (88kg)—the weight of Adrian Neville, the lightest NXT Champion

**37** ❯ The age of Samoa Joe, the oldest holder of the NXT title

**22** ❯ The age of Bo Dallas, the youngest holder of the NXT title

**14** ❯ Days—length of Samoa Joe's second NXT title reign, the shortest ever

## WOW!

**5** Out of the first seven NXT Champions have gone on to win championship gold in WWE.

## TITLE TRIVIA

By defeating Shinsuke Nakamura at *NXT TakeOver: Toronto* on November 19, 2016, Samoa Joe became the first Superstar in history to hold the NXT Championship twice.

In the main event of *NXT TakeOver: Brooklyn II* in 2016, Shinsuke Nakamura captured the NXT Championship, ending the four-month reign of Samoa Joe.

## IN DETAIL

# NEVILLE VS. SAMI ZAYN, NXT TAKEOVER: R EVOLUTION (DECEMBER 11, 2014)

For Sami Zayn, the NXT Championship was proving to be an elusive goal. After coming tantalizingly close, it seemed like he'd wasted his chances. But to earn one final shot, he put his NXT career on the line in a Title vs. Career Match. Battling back and forth, Zayn was finally able to pin Neville and win the NXT Title.

## A CHAMPION'S ENTRANCE

The flash and glitz of a spectacular ring entrance is not just limited to Superstars of *RAW* and *SmackDown*. Many NXT Champions have also created memorable ring entrances.

### SHINSUKE NAKAMURA

A VIOLINIST PLAYED HIS THEME AT *NXT TAKEOVER: BROOKLYN II*.

### FINN BÁLOR

THE DEMON KING'S ENTRANCE SET AN OMINOUS TONE AT *NXT TAKEOVER: DALLAS*.

### SAMI ZAYN

WHEN SAMI ZAYN'S MUSIC HITS, THE WWE UNIVERSE SINGS ALONG.

**BOBBY ROODE**
BOBBY ROODE HAD A FULL CHOIR PERFORM HIS ENTRANCE MUSIC LIVE.

**Q: WHO DID SETH ROLLINS DEFEAT IN THE FINALS OF THE NXT TOURNAMENT TO BE CROWNED THE FIRST-EVER NXT CHAMPION?**

**A:** Jinder Mahal.

# THE NXT CHAMPIONSHIP

**CREATED IN THE** summer of 2012, the NXT Championship has already proved to be one of the most desired titles in sports entertainment, and more than 10 Superstars have held the gold. In addition to claiming the top position in NXT, winning sets Superstars up for a bright future in WWE.

## THE REVOLUTION

NXT's Women's Division is credited with giving women's efforts in sports entertainment the respect it deserves. It all began with an eight-Superstar tournament won by Paige. At 20 years old, Paige became the first NXT Women's Champion and the youngest female champion in WWE.

### FIRST ROUND A
PAIGE DEFEATED TAMINA SNUKA.

### FIRST ROUND B
EMMA DEFEATED AKSANA.

### SEMIFINALS A
EMMA DEFEATED SUMMER RAE.

### SEMIFINALS B
PAIGE DEFEATED ALICIA FOX.

### CHAMPIONSHIP MATCH
PAIGE DEFEATED EMMA.

NXT Women's Champion Asuka stares down her challenger, veteran Superstar Mickie James, prior to their showdown at *NXT TakeOver: Toronto*.

## WOW!
## 30
Minutes—the length of the first Women's Iron Man Match. Bayley defended her title against Sasha Banks in the match for the NXT Women's Championship.

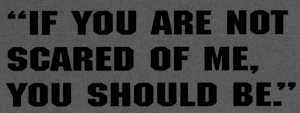

"IF YOU ARE NOT SCARED OF ME, YOU SHOULD BE."

ASUKA

## WOMEN'S CHAMPIONSHIP MOMENTS

★ **NXT TakeOver, Charlotte vs. Natalya**
In the finals of an eight-Superstar tournament, Charlotte topped veteran Natalya to become the second NXT Women's Champion of all time. Charlotte's father, the legendary Ric Flair, was on hand to celebrate.

★ **NXT TakeOver: Rival, Charlotte vs. Sasha Banks vs. Bayley vs. Becky Lynch**
This Fatal 4-Way Match included all four members of the Four Horsewomen of NXT. "The Boss" Sasha Banks emerged as the winner with her first title.

## TELL ME MORE

Asuka was one of the most feared ring warriors in Japan before arriving in NXT. General Manager William Regal proclaimed her an important signing in NXT history. Asuka floored competition with an assortment of strikes and holds, including her self-titled Asuka Lock. She remained undefeated for over a year and became the longest-reigning singles champion in NXT history—male or female.

# THE NXT WOMEN'S CHAMPIONSHIP

**SINCE ITS INTRODUCTION** in 2013, the NXT Women's Championship has been one of the most sought-after prizes in WWE. It has been the driving force for some of the most emotional rivalries, and its prestige has been elevated by the skill and enthusiasm of its amazing champions.

# IN NUMBERS ●●●

**15,589** ❯ Size of the live crowd that saw The Vaudevillains win the NXT Tag Team Championship at *NXT TakeOver: Brooklyn*, the first time the title changed hands outside the NXT Arena in Florida

**446** ❯ Combined weight in pounds (202kg) of the Revival, the first duo to win the NXT Tag Team Championship twice

**33** ❯ Age of Luke Harper when he held the title, the oldest NXT Tag Team Champion ever

**22** ❯ Age of Rezar when he held the title, the youngest NXT Tag Team Champion ever

**3** ❯ Number of teams British Ambition beat to become the first NXT Tag Team Champions

# RESULTS TABLE

NXT Tag Team Championship title changes on *NXT TakeOver* specials.

| DATE | EVENT | NEW CHAMPIONS | PREVIOUS CHAMPIONS |
|---|---|---|---|
| DECEMBER 11, 2014 | R Evolution | The Lucha Dragons | The Ascension |
| AUGUST 22, 2015 | Brooklyn | The Vaudevillains | Blake and Murphy |
| APRIL 1, 2016 | Dallas | American Alpha | The Revival |
| JUNE 8, 2016 | The End | The Revival | American Alpha |
| NOVEMBER 19, 2016 | Toronto | #DIY | The Revival |
| JANUARY 28, 2017 | San Antonio | Authors of Pain | #DIY |

## Q: WHICH TWO TAG TEAMS WON THE *SMACKDOWN* TAG TEAM CHAMPIONSHIP IN 2016 AFTER PREVIOUSLY HOLDING THE NXT TAG TEAM CHAMPIONSHIP?

**A:** American Alpha and the Wyatt Family.

# THE NXT TAG TEAM CHAMPIONSHIP

**SINCE THE BEGINNING** of 2013, NXT Superstar pairings have fought to capture the NXT Tag Team Championship. In the first four years of the title's history, 10 different duos have captured the gold, including The Ascension, The Lucha Dragons, and American Alpha.

The Ascension combined raw power and clever double-team moves to defeat opponents Kalisto and El Local at *NXT TakeOver*, in May 2014.

## WOW! 3

Championships—with his two Tag Team Championship reigns and NXT title win, Neville is the only Superstar to win so many in NXT.

## IN DETAIL

### THE ASCENSION VS. THE LUCHA DRAGONS, *NXT TAKEOVER: FATAL 4-WAY* (SEPTEMBER 11, 2014)

The reign of the NXT Tag Team Champions, The Ascension, was approaching one calendar year—all they needed to do was to turn back top challengers The Lucha Dragons at *Fatal 4-Way*. But the Mexican Superstars were able to upset the champions and end their record-setting reign.

## THE SECOND ANNUAL DUSTY CLASSIC

On November 19, 2016, The Authors of Pain, led by manager Paul Ellering, ripped their way through a field of 15 other competitors to win the second Dusty Classic.

### FIRST ROUND
DEFEATED THE BOLLYWOOD BOYS.

### QUARTERFINALS
DEFEATED NO WAY JOSE AND RICH SWANN.

### SEMIFINALS
DEFEATED #DIY.

Honoring the legendary American Dream, the finals of the first-ever Dusty Rhodes Classic took place at *NXT: TakeOver: Respect* on October 7, 2015.

### FINALS
DEFEATED TM-61.

# THE DUSTY CLASSIC

**AFTER A HALL OF FAME** in-ring career, Dusty Rhodes (AKA the American Dream) continued to give back to sports entertainment by training and leading the next generation of Superstars at NXT. After his tragic passing in 2015, NXT decided to honor his memory by holding an annual tag team tournament named after him.

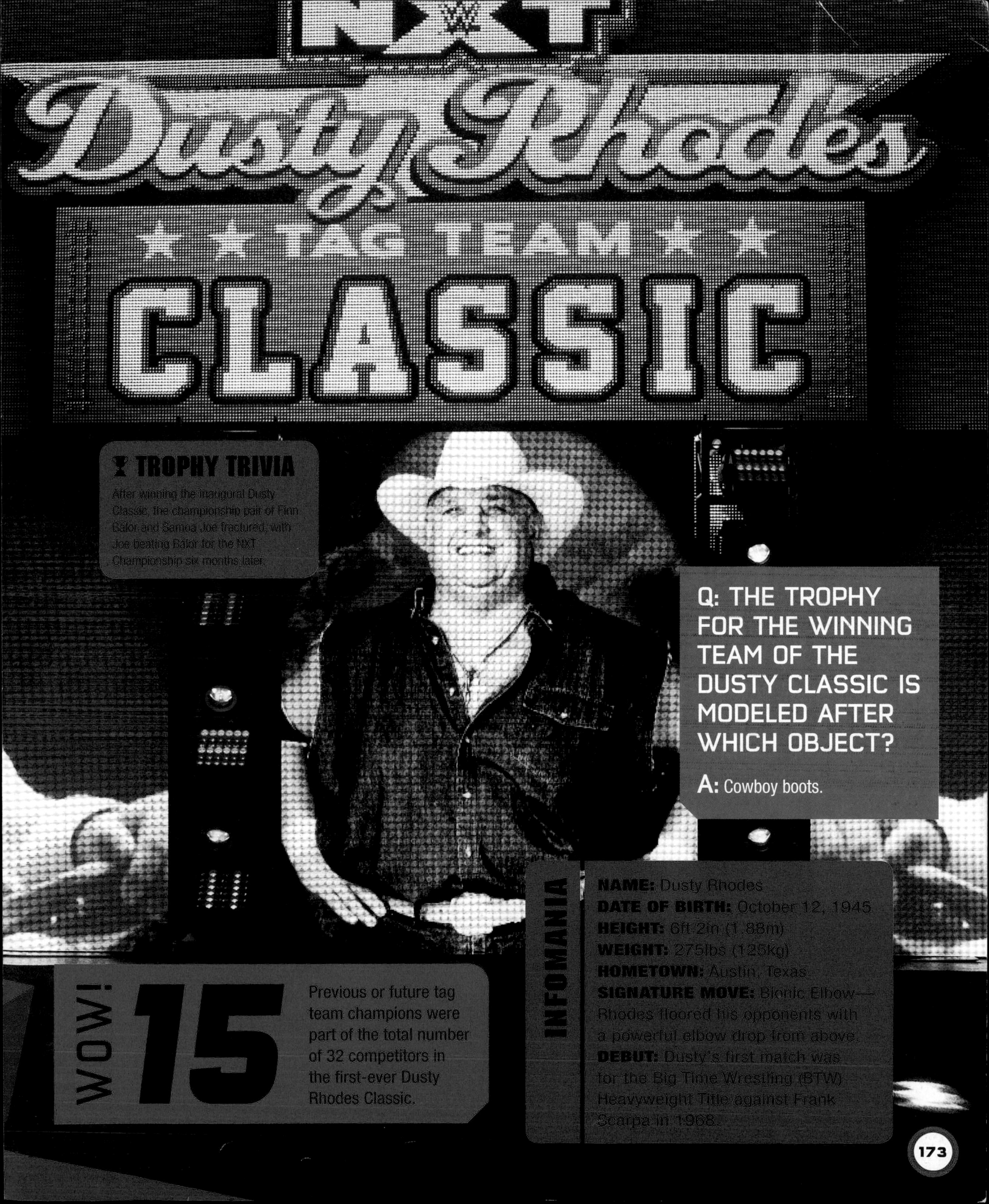

# NXT DUSTY RHODES TAG TEAM CLASSIC

**Q: THE TROPHY FOR THE WINNING TEAM OF THE DUSTY CLASSIC IS MODELED AFTER WHICH OBJECT?**

**A:** Cowboy boots.

**WOW! 15**

Previous or future tag team champions were part of the total number of 32 competitors in the first-ever Dusty Rhodes Classic.

**INFOMANIA**

**NAME:** Dusty Rhodes
**DATE OF BIRTH:** October 12, 1945
**HEIGHT:** 6ft 2in (1.88m)
**WEIGHT:** 275lbs (125kg)
**HOMETOWN:** Austin, Texas
**SIGNATURE MOVE:** Bionic Elbow—Rhodes floored his opponents with a powerful elbow drop from above.
**DEBUT:** Dusty's first match was for the Big Time Wrestling (BTW) Heavyweight Title against Frank Scarpa in 1968.

SmackDown Live General Manager Daniel Bryan and Commissioner Shane McMahon speak of their vision to create a "land of opportunity" for Superstars.

## THE 2016 WWE DRAFT, *SMACKDOWN LIVE* (JULY 19, 2016)

In 2016, WWE held its first draft in five years on the premier of *SmackDown Live*. From the beginning, it was clear WWE would never be the same again. In round one, *SmackDown Live* claimed the WWE Champion Dean Ambrose while *RAW* seized WWE Women's Champion Charlotte. By the end of the night, WWE Tag Team Champions The New Day and United States Champion Rusev were property of *RAW* while Intercontinental Champion The Miz joined *SmackDown*.

## Q: WHO WAS THE FIRST-EVER DRAFT PICK IN *RAW* HISTORY?

**A:** Undertaker. After Mr. McMahon selected The Rock to move to *SmackDown* with the first pick, WWE co-owner Ric Flair countered by snagging Undertaker for *RAW*. Undertaker was furious, since he and Flair were bitter rivals at the time. Months later, Undertaker got his wish and moved over to *SmackDown*, where he would become the brand's cornerstone Superstar.

WOW!

**2**

The number of picks for John Cena in the 2011 WWE Draft—the first Superstar to be drafted twice in one night. Cena went to *SmackDown* with the first pick and then back to *RAW* with the final pick!

## "IT'S TIME TO SHAKE THINGS UP AGAIN!"

MR. MCMAHON

Finn Bálor became part of history when he became the first-ever draft pick from the NXT brand.

## IN NUMBERS ● ● ●

**59** ❯ Superstars drafted to *RAW* and *SmackDown Live* as part of the 2016 draft

**6** ❯ NXT Superstars drafted in 2016

**5** ❯ Number of times a United States Champion has been drafted

**2** ❯ Commentators have been drafted, Jim Ross and Michael Cole (2008)

**1** ❯ During the 2016 draft, Heath Slater was the one Superstar from the main roster who wasn't drafted

# THE WWE DRAFT

**ONE OF THE** most unsettling nights on the WWE calendar is the WWE Draft—when Superstars are selected to be exclusive property of one of two WWE brands—*RAW* or *SmackDown*. The draft has forced champions to face unknown rivals, tag teams to split up, and new alliances to form.

# WWE BEYOND THE RING

## 07

# WWE HISTORY

**SINCE ITS CREATION IN 1963**, WWE has slowly grown from a northeastern wrestling territory to a global sports-entertainment powerhouse. WWE now offers weekly television shows, historical content, and new specials on the WWE Network, plus several live events.

## "THEN. NOW. FOREVER."
WWE SLOGAN

**WOW!**

## 7

Of the nine WWE Championship title changes in the first 25 years of its history happened in Madison Square Garden, New York.

## LEADERBOARD

Largest attendance numbers at WWE events.

| EVENT | DATE | LOCATION | ATTENDANCE |
|---|---|---|---|
| WrestleMania 32 | April 3, 2016 | AT&T Stadium, Arlington, Texas | 101,763 |
| SummerSlam 1992 | August 29, 1992 | Wembley Stadium, London, England | 80,355 |
| The Big Event | August 28, 1986 | CNE Stadium, Toronto, Canada | 64,100 |
| Royal Rumble 1997 | January 19, 1997 | The Alamodome, San Antonio, Texas | 60,477 |
| Global Warning | August 10, 2002 | Colonial Stadium, Melbourne, Australia | 56,734 |
| Tribute to the Troops 2010 | December 11, 2010 | Fort Hood, Texas | 50,000 |
| Showdown at Shea | August 9, 1980 | Shea Stadium, New York, New York | 36,295 |
| Monday Night RAW | January 31, 1997 | Skydome, Toronto, Canada | 25,628 |
| King of the Ring | July 8, 1985 | Sullivan Stadium, Foxboro, Massachusetts | 23,000 |
| Survivor Series | November 26, 1987 | Richfield Coliseum, Richfield, Ohio | 21,300 |

## WWE HEADQUARTERS

TITAN TOWER IS THE CENTER FOR WWE CORPORATE BUSINESS.

## THE HOME OF WWE

WWE Headquarters is located in Stamford, Connecticut. Titan Tower was established in 1991 and has been used as the location for behind-the-scenes segments and live action.

WWE Chairman Vince McMahon welcomes a then-record 93,173 members of the WWE Universe to *WrestleMania III* in the Pontiac Silverdome in Michigan.

## BOARDROOM

SOME OF THE MOST IMPORTANT DECISIONS ABOUT THE DIRECTION OF *RAW* AND *SMACKDOWN* ARE MADE IN THE WWE BOARD ROOM.

## CORPORATE WORKOUT

WHEN IN TOWN, MANY WWE SUPERSTARS WORK OUT IN THE CORPORATE OFFICE'S STATE-OF-THE-ART GYM.

## SUPER FOOD

WWE'S BIGGEST SUPERSTARS LOOK OVER EMPLOYEES AND VISITORS IN THE CORPORATE CAFETERIA.

## KEY DATES

**April 25, 1963:** Buddy Rogers is crowned the first WWE Champion in history.

**May 11, 1985:** *Saturday Night's Main Event* launches its inaugural show, the first time WWE ever aired on network television.

**August 29, 1992:** *SummerSlam 1992* takes place in Wembley Stadium, London, England, the first pay-per-view event to take place outside of North America.

**March 25, 2002:** Through its first-ever draft, WWE splits its talent across *RAW* and *SmackDown* in its brand extension.

**Q: WHICH CABLE NETWORK AIRED WWE'S *BRAWL TO END IT ALL* IN 1984 AND *THE WAR TO SETTLE THE SCORE* IN 1985?**

A: MTV.

# 7,000

Hours of in-demand programming are available on the WWE Network at any time of the day.

## Q: WHAT WAS THE FIRST PAY-PER-VIEW EVENT TO AIR ON THE WWE NETWORK?

**A:** *WrestleMania 30.*

The WWE Universe can count on finding in-depth analysis of WWE's biggest events on the WWE Network.

## RESULTS TABLE

Popular out-of-the-ring shows that are aired on the WWE Network.

| WWE SHOW | DESCRIPTION | NUMBER OF EPISODES |
|---|---|---|
| WWE COUNTDOWN | Ranks the top 10 entries on topics near and dear to the WWE Universe, such as ring gear or trash talk. | 34 |
| WWE SLAM CITY | An animated show featuring the WWE Superstars holding down day jobs. | 26 |
| TABLE FOR 3 | A trio of current or former Superstars discuss their time in sports entertainment. | 17 |
| SWERVED | WWE Superstars play pranks on each other. | 16 |
| THE EDGE AND CHRISTIAN SHOW THAT TOTALLY REEKS OF AWESOMENESS | Comedy variety show featuring the former tag team champions. | 12 |
| WWE LEGENDS HOUSE | Eight WWE legends live in a house together. | 10 |

## IN NUMBERS ●●●

**1.49 million** ➤ Number of subscribers to the WWE Network as of December 2016

**220** ➤ Number of countries where the WWE Network is aired

**15** ➤ Number of *NXT TakeOver* specials aired on the WWE Network as of April 2017

# WWE NETWORK

## TROPHY TRIVIA

The WWE Network won a Cynopsis Sports Media award for most "Over-The-Top Content" in 2016.

**LAUNCHED IN 2014**, the WWE Network provides sports-entertainment programming for an insatiable WWE Universe. Whether a live feed or in-demand programming from an extensive library of WWE, WCW, ECW, AWA, and WCCW matches, there is always something worth watching.

**JOHN CENA AND DOLPH ZIGGLER**
CENA AND DOLPH DEFEATED KING BARRETT AND KANE.

## FIREWORKS IN JAPAN

*Beast in the East* was a WWE Network special that aired on Independence Day 2015, and the first WWE event to be broadcast live from Japan.

## NIKKI BELLA VS. TAMINA AND PAIGE

IN A TRIPLE THREAT MATCH, NIKKI BELLA WON THE DIVAS CHAMPIONSHIP.

## IN DETAIL

### LEGENDS WITH JBL (SEPTEMBER 21, 2015)

Former WWE Champion JBL launched a new show on the WWE Network, interviewing controversial figures on hard-hitting topics. His first-ever episode featured former WCW President Eric Bischoff, who detailed how he tried to put WWE out of business and what went wrong.

**BROCK VS. KOFI**
BROCK LESNAR DEFEATED KOFI KINGSTON.

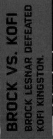

**FINN BÁLOR VS. KEVIN OWENS**
BÁLOR DEFEATED OWENS FOR THE NXT CHAMPIONSHIP.

★ **The leprechaun in *Leprechaun: Origins* (2014)**
In a remote cabin in the Irish countryside, four college students encounter a terrifying legend. To make matters worse, they become locked inside the cabin with the bloodthirsty creature, played by Superstar Hornswoggle.

★ **A.J. in *Inside Out* (2011)**
In this starring role, Triple H portrays A.J., an ex-con who is unwillingly pulled back into the criminal underbelly of New Orleans. He finds himself in the crosshairs of one of the city's most notorious gangsters.

★ **Jack Conrad in *The Condemned* (2007)**
A defiant prisoner, played by Stone Cold Steve Austin, is forced to fight his fellow inmates to the death in a sadistic game arranged by an unscrupulous producer looking to achieve high ratings by broadcasting the contest on the internet.

★ **Jacob Goodnight in *See No Evil* (2006)**
Played by Kane, Jacob Goodnight is a menacing killer lurking in the rundown Blackwell Hotel. When a group of youths are tasked with fixing up the premises, it leads to devastating consequences and the disturbing truth behind Goodnight's origin is revealed.

## IN DETAIL

### THE ROCK

No WWE Superstar has electrified the silver screen quite like The Rock. First impressing in *The Mummy Returns* in 2001, The Rock has evolved into a mainstream celebrity and a Hollywood icon. Among the thirty-plus movies he has starred in are *Hercules*, *San Andreas*, *Race to Witch Mountain*, *Walking Tall*, and the *Fast & Furious* series. In 2016, The Rock was the world's highest-grossing actor, according to *Forbes*, and his popularity and success continues to rise.

# WWE STUDIOS

**WWE SUPERSTARS** often take their talents to the silver screen. WWE Studios opened in 2002 and, since then, the WWE Universe has been able to enjoy their heroes in a variety of roles in film genres ranging from action and horror to comedy, drama, and much more.

# 48

Number of films that have featured WWE Superstars since WWE Studios was founded.

Big Show starred as Walter Crunk, a 35-year-old orphan, in the movie *Knucklehead*.

### THE MARINE 5: BATTLEGROUND (2017)

THE MIZ PLAYS CARTER ONCE AGAIN AS HE TAKES ON A BIKER GANG CONSISTING OF SUPERSTARS CURTIS AXEL, HEATH SLATER, BO DALLAS, AND NAOMI.

### THE MARINE 4: MOVING TARGET (2015)

NOW A TOPLINE SECURITY GUARD, JAKE CARTER (THE MIZ) AND DAWES (SUMMER RAE) TAKE DOWN A CORRUPT DEFENSE CORPORATION.

## THE MARINE FRANCHISE

John Cena shone in his first movie role as ex-Marine John Triton in 2006. Since then, Cena has tackled several diverse acting roles while *The Marine* has become a reoccurring staple for WWE Studios, and has featured several WWE Superstars.

### THE MARINE (2006)

JOHN TRITON (CENA) IS TASKED WITH RESCUING HIS WIFE FROM A GANG OF JEWEL THIEVES.

### THE MARINE 2 (2009)

MARINE SNIPER JOE LINWOOD (TED DIBIASE) COMBATS TERRORISTS WHO HAVE SEIZED A LUXURIOUS RESORT.

### THE MARINE 3: HOMEFRONT (2013)

A JOYOUS HOMECOMING FOR SGT. JAKE CARTER (THE MIZ) TURNS SOUR WHEN CARTER MUST SAVE THE CITY FROM AN EXPLOSIVE ATTACK.

> ## "WE ALL HAVE ONE COMMON GOAL IN WWE AND THAT IS TO MAKE DREAMS COME TRUE."
> JOHN CENA

## WOW! 500

Number of wishes John Cena has granted for the Make-A-Wish© Foundation—far more than any other professional athlete.

# WWE IN THE COMMUNITY

**DESPITE THEIR TIRELESS** schedule, WWE Superstars always have time to lend a helping hand. Wherever their travels take them, they are leaders in the community, eager to lend support to those in need and help address important social issues.

John Cena, Nikki Bella, and Stephanie McMahon at the USO-Metro Annual Awards Dinner in Washington, D.C., a black-tie event in honor of the US Armed Forces.

## WRESTLEMANIA READING CHALLENGE

KIDS AND THEIR FAMILIES COMMIT TO READING EVERY DAY FOR A CHANCE TO GO TO *WRESTLEMANIA*.

## RISE ABOVE CANCER

EACH YEAR, WWE JOINS THE EFFORT TO END BREAST CANCER.

## BE A STAR

THIS ANTI-BULLYING CRUSADE SENDS A MESSAGE OF RESPECT.

## TRIBUTE TO THE TROOPS

SINCE 2003, WWE SUPERSTARS HAVE PERFORMED FOR TROOPS AT HOME AND ABROAD.

## GIVING BACK

WWE partners with several charitable organizations to make a positive impact. Through TV, social media, and other platforms, it also encourages the WWE Universe and the public at large to take action and help those in need.

# TOTAL DIVAS

## 🏆 TROPHY TRIVIA

*Total Divas* was twice nominated for the "Choice TV: Reality Show" award at the Teen Choice Awards in 2014 and 2016, losing out to *Keeping Up with the Kardashians*.

**THE WWE UNIVERSE** simply cannot get enough of the lives of their favorite WWE Superstars. Since July 2013, they have been able to follow the out-of-the-ring exploits of some female Superstars thanks to the TV show *Total Divas*, which airs on the E! Network.

## RESULTS TABLE

*Total Divas* focuses on female Superstars' lives outside the ring, including their romantic relationships. These cast members have Superstar significant others.

| SUPERSTAR | SIGNIFICANT OTHER |
|---|---|
| BRIE BELLA | Daniel Bryan |
| NIKKI BELLA | John Cena |
| NATALYA | Tyson Kidd |
| NAOMI | Jimmy Uso |
| RENEE YOUNG | Dean Ambrose |
| LANA | Rusev |
| MARYSE | The Miz |

## WOW!

**81**

Total number of *Total Divas* episodes that have aired in the show's six seasons since July 2013.

## Q: WHICH WWE SUPERSTAR PROPOSED MARRIAGE TO HIS GIRLFRIEND ON THE SEASON 1 FINALE OF *TOTAL DIVAS*?

**A:** Daniel Bryan proposed to Brie Bella.

*Total Divas* goes behind the scenes of the hectic personal and professional lives of some of WWE's toughest female Superstars.

## LEADERBOARD

Championships won by *Total Divas* cast members.

| SUPERSTAR | NUMBER OF TITLES |
| --- | --- |
| Nikki Bella | 2 |
| Paige | 2 |
| Maryse | 2 |
| Naomi | 2 |
| Natalya | 1 |
| Alicia Fox | 1 |
| Brie Bella | 1 |

## IN DETAIL

## TEAM *TOTAL DIVAS* VS. TEAM B.A.D. AND BLONDE, *WRESTLEMANIA 32* PRE-SHOW (APRIL 3, 2016)

Team B.A.D. and Blonde, consisting of Lana, Naomi, Tamina, Emma, and Summer Rae, teamed up to face five members of the *Total Divas* cast at *WrestleMania 32* in a 10-woman tag team match. Brie Bella was able to pin Naomi and claim victory for her and fellow castmates Paige, Natalya, Eva Marie, and Alicia Fox.

# ★ BEST-EVER...

## WWE PRODUCT FACTS

**★ Stephanie's debut**
Many note Stephanie McMahon's WWE debut as the time she was kidnapped by Undertaker. However, her first job with her father's company was modeling Superstar t-shirts for the WWE merchandise catalogue.

**★ Sting arrives**
WWE unveiled its first-ever Sting action figure at the 2014 San Diego ComicCon, then shocked fans by unveiling the real Sting! This marked his first public appearance in WWE over his 30-year sports-entertainment career.

**★ Ultimate Warrior returns**
After being estranged for nearly 20 years, Ultimate Warrior's emotional return to WWE began when those who pre-ordered the *2K14* video game were able to play as Warrior.

**★ Rise and Fall of ECW documentary**
Consumer products played a role in WWE's revival of ECW in 2006. DVD releases such as the top-selling *Rise and Fall of ECW* documentary proved that fans still had an appetite for the extreme brand of sports entertainment.

Superstar t-shirts, pendants, championship titles, event programs, and more are displayed at *Wrestlemania 31* Axxess in 2015.

## "...AND YOU CAN FIND ALL THESE GREAT GIFT-GIVING ITEMS NOW ON WWESHOP.COM!"

D-GENERATION X

## Q: WHAT WAS THE NAME OF WWE'S FIRST MUSIC ALBUM?

**A:** *The Wrestling Album.* Released in 1985, at the height of the Rock 'n' Wrestling movement, the record cover featured Mr. McMahon and several WWE Superstars. Among the many entrance themes included were Junkyard Dog's "*Grab Them Cakes*" and Hillbilly Jim's "*Don't Go Messin' With a Country Boy,*" each performed by the Superstars themselves.

# LICENSING AND MERCHANDISE

**THE WWE UNIVERSE** wear their loyalty on their sleeves, sometimes quite literally! WWE is constantly rolling out new products that chronicle the history and excitement of WWE's biggest events, including apparel, video games, action figures, and books.

## AWESOME PRODUCTS

WWE's product range includes traditional merchandise, such as trading cards and posters. But there are also some creative novelty items that have really made an impact on shelves and will be remembered fondly as part of WWE history.

## ICE-CREAM BARS

CM PUNK FAMOUSLY DEMANDED THE RETURN OF THESE 1980'S TREATS, TO NO AVAIL.

THE SUPERSTARS OF WRESTLING PRESENT

**ICE CREAMANIA!**

TASTE THE BARS OF THE SUPERSTARS

Hey fans! Grab the champion of ice cream bars!

## WRESTLING BUDDIES

THESE SOFT SUPERSTAR LIKENESSES WERE REVIVED BY MATTEL AS BRAWLIN' BUDDIES.

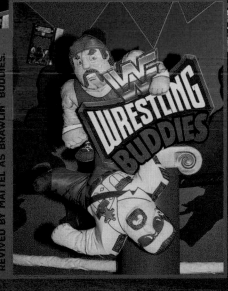

## BOOTY O'S

THE NEW DAY'S CEREAL BECAME A REALITY IN 2016 WITH THE SLOGAN "THEY MAKE SURE YOU AIN'T BOOTY!"

## WOW!

# 25

Number of WWE books that have made it onto the *New York Times Bestseller List*, including Daniel Bryan's autobiography *YES!* and DK's *WWE 50*.

## THE BATTLE FOR THE DIVAS CHAMPIONSHIP

The fiercely fought Divas Championship passed from one *Diva Search* or NXT competitor to another on several occasions.

**DECEMBER 22, 2008**
MARYSE DEFEATED MICHELLE MCCOOL.

**SEPTEMBER 16, 2012**
EVE TORRES DEFEATED LAYLA.

**JANUARY 14, 2013**
KAITLYN DEFEATED EVE TORRES.

**JUNE 16, 2013**
AJ LEE DEFEATED KAITLYN.

The finalists in the sixth season of *Tough Enough* hope to impress the judges.

# FINDING THE NEXT SUPERSTARS

**ONE OF THE MOST DESIRED** opportunities in all of sports entertainment is the chance to make it to the WWE roster and become a WWE Superstar. Men and women can demonstrate why they should be the ones to make the roster on seasons of *Tough Enough*, *Diva Search*, and NXT.

**Q: SEASON 1 *TOUGH ENOUGH* WINNER MAVEN SHOCKINGLY ELIMINATED WHICH MULTI-TIME WWE CHAMPION FROM THE 2002 *ROYAL RUMBLE*?**

**A:** Undertaker.

# RESULTS TABLE
Winners and runner-ups of NXT.

| SEASON | WINNER | RUNNER-UP |
|---|---|---|
| NXT SEASON 1 | Wade Barrett | David Otunga |
| NXT SEASON 2 | Kaval | Michael McGillicutty |
| NXT SEASON 3 | Kaitlyn | Naomi |
| NXT SEASON 4 | Johnny Curtis | Brodus Clay |
| NXT SEASON 5 | Derrick Bateman, Darren Young, Titus O'Neil | Connor O'Brien |

## TITLE TRIVIA

By winning the WWE Women's Championship at *Vengeance 2007*, Candice Michelle became the first *Diva Search* contestant to win a championship in WWE.

## WOW! 73

Combined number of WWE championships that contestants on *Tough Enough*, *Diva Search*, and NXT have gone on to win.

## IN NUMBERS ● ● ●

**$1,000,000** ❯ Value of the contract won by the fourth season of *Tough Enough* winner, Daniel Puder

**7,000** ❯ Number of women who applied to compete in the first *Diva Search*

**4,000** ❯ Number of competitors who sent in audition tapes for the first season of *Tough Enough*

**25** ❯ Number of matches won by Titus O'Neil in *NXT: Redemption* season five—an NXT record

# ★ BEST-EVER...

## ▶ INTERNATIONAL INCIDENTS

★ **The Shield Strikes, England (April 2013)**
The Shield arrived in spectacular style at the O2 Arena in London, England—in a helicopter for their match against Undertaker and Team Hell No. Days later on *SmackDown*, the trio went after Undertaker again and put him through a table with a Triple Powerbomb move.

★ **JBL vs. Godzilla, Japan (February 2005)**
WWE Champion JBL was accidentally shot with a tranquilizer on *SmackDown* in Japan. Feeling the effects, JBL talked trash to an inflatable version of Godzilla. When his rival Big Show came down to stop the charade, JBL snapped out of it and attacked him.

★ **The Milan Miracle, Italy (April 2007)**
During a *RAW* episode in Milan, Italy, Mr. McMahon issued an open challenge for anyone to step in the ring with Intercontinental Champion Umaga. WWE Universe member Santino Marella hopped the barricade and shockingly defeated the giant Samoan.

Sasha Banks, Alicia Fox, and Bayley salute fans in Strasbourg, France during the November 2016 European tour.

## IN NUMBERS ● ● ●

**73** ❯ International *RAW* and *SmackDown Live* shows in 2016

**15** ❯ International NXT shows in 2016

**2** ❯ Two-week European tours per year

**1st** ❯ WWE Live event in China was held on September 10, 2016

WOW!

# 320

Number of live events WWE Superstars perform in around the world every year.

## SUPERSTARS ABROAD

Traveling the world has its perks. Superstars take care of business in the ring first, but they always find time to take in their surroundings.

### NEWCASTLE, ENGLAND (NOVEMBER 2015)
BAYLEY, ALEXA BLISS, AND EMMA ENJOY THE BRITISH COUNTRYSIDE.

### CAIRO, EGYPT (OCTOBER 2012)
SEVERAL WWE SUPERSTARS VISIT THE PYRAMIDS PRIOR TO A LIVE EVENT.

### ROME, ITALY (APRIL 2012)
DAVID OTUNGA SHOWS OFF HIS MUSCLES OUTSIDE THE ROMAN COLOSSEUM.

# TOURING THE WORLD

**LIFE IN WWE** is non-stop: Superstars are on the road year-round, bringing their dynamic form of sports entertainment to a different city virtually every night. No matter where in the world they may be, the WWE Universe can see some of the biggest Superstars in an arena nearby.

## RESULTS TABLE

Famous supporters who have become WWE competitors at events.

| FAMOUS SUPPORTER | EVENT | DETAILS |
| --- | --- | --- |
| STEPHEN AMELL (ACTOR) | SummerSlam 2015 (August 23, 2015) | Amell teamed with Neville to defeat Stardust and King Barrett in tag team action. |
| KEVIN FEDERLINE (RAPPER) | WWE RAW (January 1, 2007) | Former husband of Britney Spears, Federline stunned John Cena in a match on New Year's Day. |
| JAY LENO (TV TALK SHOW HOST) | Road Wild 1998 (August 8, 1998) | Leno and Diamond Dallas Page beat Hollywood Hogan and Eric Bischoff. |
| MARIA MENOUNOS (TV HOST) | WrestleMania XXVIII (April 1, 2012) | Menounos and Kelly Kelly defeated Eve Torres and Beth Phoenix in a Tag Team Match. |
| DENNIS RODMAN AND KARL MALONE (BASKETBALL PLAYERS) | Bash at the Beach 1998 (July 12, 1998) | Hollywood Hogan partnered with Rodman to beat Diamond Dallas Page and Karl Malone in a Tag Team Match. |
| LAWRENCE TAYLOR (AMERICAN FOOTBALL PLAYER) | WrestleMania XI (April 2, 1995) | Taylor pinned Bam Bam Bigelow in the main event at WrestleMania XI. |

## "WE PUT SMILES ON PEOPLE'S FACES."

MR. McMAHON REFERRING TO
THE WWE UNIVERSE

## POPULAR WWE UNIVERSE CHANTS

**"U-S-A! U-S-A!":** "Hacksaw" Jim Duggan's entrance would spark patriotic fervor in the WWE Universe.

**"YES! YES! YES!":** Fans used the chant to celebrate Daniel Bryan's moves and wins.

**"WHAT?":** Audiences tried to stay in the good graces of the Texas Rattle Snake, Stone Cold Steve Austin, so they would chant "WHAT?" whenever a rival would pause during a speech.

**"WOOOOOO!":** Ric Flair is so associated with the Reverse Knife Edge Chest Chop that to this day, when any Superstar smacks the chest of an opponent, the crowd yells Flair's signature "Wooooooo!"

**Q: *WRESTLEMANIA 2* TOOK PLACE IN WHICH THREE CITIES?**

**A:** Uniondale, New York; Chicago, Illinois; and Los Angeles, California.

## 🏆 TROPHY TRIVIA

In 1998, Minnesota voters elected Jesse Ventura Governor of their state, making him the first former WWE Superstar to hold that level of office.

The WWE Universe's eagerness to attend live events makes events like the *Royal Rumble* the hottest ticket in town.

194

# THE WWE UNIVERSE

**THE LIFEBLOOD** of WWE is its passionate fan base. Generations of fans have cheered on their heroes, booed villains, and brought an incredible intensity to all live events. Nothing matches the excitement of seeing the biggest and best Superstars battle each other for the ultimate title win.

**WOW!**

## 1

Number of minutes it took for tickets to *WrestleMania 21* in Los Angeles to sell out, making it the fastest-selling event in Staples Center history.

### GIGANTIC SUPPORT
FANS HAVE BROUGHT SIGNS TO WWE EVENTS FOR DECADES.

### THE CESARO SECTION
FANS USE SIGNS TO CREATE A CESARO SECTION AT EVERY EVENT.

### NWO LOYALTY
THE NWO ALWAYS HAD AN AVID FAN BASE DISPLAYING SIGNS.

## SIGNS OF THE WWE UNIVERSE

The WWE Universe display signs that proudly announce messages about their favorite Superstars and factions.

# GLOSSARY

**2 OUT OF 3 FALLS MATCH:** A bout in which one individual or team must record two decisions (pinfall, submission, TKO/technical knockout, disqualification, or count out) in order to win the match.

**AWA:** Abbreviation for American Wrestling Alliance, a Midwestern promotion based in Minneapolis that competed with WWE for decades before ceasing operations in 1991.

**DECISION:** Also known as a fall. Any way in which a competitor can emerge victorious in the match, including pinfall, submission, TKO, disqualification, count out, or referee stoppage. Most matches require only one decision to end the match, but specialty matches may have other rules.

**DRAW:** A match that ends without either side recording a positive decision.

**ECW:** Abbreviation for Extreme Championship Wrestling, a popular wrestling promotion in the 1990s and early 2000s that built a rapid and loyal fan base. ECW was known for its unique and intense matches.

**FALL:** See decision.

**FATAL 4-WAY MATCH:** A bout featuring four individuals or teams, each trying to secure a victory over the other three teams. In a standard Fatal 4-Way Match, the first decision ends the contest. In an Fatal 4-Way Elimination Match, a victor is not determined until all other individuals or teams have lost.

**IRON MAN MATCH:** A contest set to a specific time limit (often 30 or 60 minutes) in which the individual or team that records the most decisions within the total time of the match wins the bout.

**LAST MAN STANDING MATCH:** A match in which a victory can only be achieved if the winner records a decision and then their opponent cannot get up within a 10 count administered by the official.

**MAIN EVENT:** The final match of a wrestling event's lineup, usually a championship match or some other marquee bout.

**NWA:** Abbreviation for National Wrestling Alliance, a grouping of national and international wrestling promotions that worked together for most of the 20th century.

**PIN:** A competitor covers an opponent and holds down his or her shoulders while an official slaps his hand on the mat three times.

Shane McMahon leaps from the top of a steel cage during a Hell in a Cell Match at *WrestleMania 32*, aiming to land on his opponent, Undertaker, and win the contest.

**PAY-PER-VIEW:** A special lineup of matches that aired on cable and satellite networks for an extra fee. These special events now air on the WWE Network. Popular examples include *WrestleMania*, *SummerSlam*, *Royal Rumble*, and *Survivor Series*.

**ROUND-ROBIN TOURNAMENT:** A group of Superstars compete against each other in a series of one-on-one matches. Either the best record wins the tournament, or the two best records advance to a final match.

**STABLE:** A group of multiple competitors that often work together to achieve common goals and eliminate common enemies. Stables are often led by a manager. Successful historical stables include the Four Horsemen, the New World Order, and D-Generation X.

**SUBMISSION HOLD:** A maneuver that causes an opponent pain, with the object of forcing the opponent to give up the match.

**TITLE:** Also known as a championship, a title is a physical championship belt awarded to the top competitor in a group of individuals. That individual is then expected to defend that championship title against other competitors in title matches. WWE titles include the WWE Championship, Universal Championship, Intercontinental Championship, United States Championship, Cruiserweight Championship, and the *RAW* and *SmackDown* Women's and Tag Team Championships.

**TITLE-FOR-TITLE MATCH:** A championship bout in which both competitors are champions before the match, and both titles are on the line. The victor emerges as a double champion.

**TLC MATCH:** A bout in which the use of tables, ladders, and chairs are legally allowed. A championship title or some other object is suspended above the center of the ring and to win the match, a competitor must position a ladder under the object, climb the ladder, and retrieve the object.

**UNIFICATION MATCH:** A championship bout in which both competitors are champions before the match. Unlike a title-for-title match, where the winner becomes a double champion, the two titles are combined into a single championship after the unification match, and the victor of the contest is the new champion of the unified championship.

**WCW:** Abbreviation for World Championship Wrestling, a national wrestling promotion that competed with WWE for sports entertainment supremacy for years before the company went out of business in early 2001.

# INDEX

Page numbers in **bold** refer to main entries.

#DIY 170, 172

## A

Aksana 168
Ambrose, Dean 42, 43, **52–3**, 87, 95, 140, 148, 150–51, 153, 174, 186
American Alpha 97, 125, 165, 170, 171
Amore, Enzo 97, 122, 123, 170
Anderson, Arn 19, 112
Anderson, Karl 96, 122
André the Giant **6–7**, 9, 11, 19, 22, 66, 121, 139
Angle, Kurt 30, 34, 48, 80, 98, 119, 125, 148, 153
Animal 19, 116–17, 145
announcers **130–31**, 162, 175
The Ascension 123, 165, 171
Asuka 161, 168, 169
Austin, Stone Cold Steve 20–21, 27, 67, 81, 87, 99, 130, 136, 137, 139, 182, 194
The Authority 37, 51, **128–9**
The Authors of Pain 160, 165, 170, 172
Axel, Curtis 42, 105, 183

## B

Backlund, Bob 76, 86
Bálor, Finn 76, 77, 92, 164, 165, 167, 173, 175, 181
Banks, Sasha 61, **70–71**, 75, 113, 135, 164, 168, 169, 192
Barrett, Wade 56, 191
The Basham Brothers 125
Batista 37, 57, 100, 125, 130, 143, 149
*Battlebowl: The Lethal Lottery* 144
Bayley 61, 70, 113, 162, 164, 168, 169, 192, 193
Bearer, Paul 39, 80, 81
Bella, Brie 61, 186, 187
Bella, Nikki 60, 78, 79, 181, 185, 186, 187

Benjamin, Shelton 52, 89
Benoit, Chris 52, 94, 112, 125
Big Cass 59, 92, 97, 122, 123, 170
Big E 105
Big Show 6, 55, **66–7**, 68, 80, 95, 106, 114, 124, 129, 150, 152, 153, 156, 157, 183, 192
Bischoff, Eric 110, 155, 181
Bliss, Alexa 60, 75, 78, 79, 148, 193
Bockwinkel, Nick 30, 121
Bollywood Boys 172
The Boogeyman 72–3
Booker, King 98, 146
Booker T 41, 94, 95, 126, 130
The Brain Busters 121
Breezango 97, 123
Breeze, Tyler 42, 164, 165
The Briscoe Brothers 126
British Ambition 170
The British Bulldogs 28, 126
Bryan, Daniel 37, **48**, 52, 62, 63, 64, 69, 109, 139, 141, 147, 150, 174, 186, 187, 189, 194
Bundy, King Kong 8, 11, 120

## C

Cara, Sin 76, 88
Carlito 59, 109
Cena, John 12, **34–5**, 38, 40, 43, 50, 59, 68, 94, 95, 108, 129, 139, 140, 141, 142, 147, 150, 153, 174, 181, 183, 184, 185, 186
Cesaro 52, 63, 69, 77, 96, 105, 195
chants 194
charity work **184–5**
Charlotte **60–61**, 70, 71, 74, 90, 101, 113, 135, 151, 169, 174
Christian 114, 118–19, 156
Chyna 90, 98, 106
Cole, Michael 130, 138, 175
The Colossal Connection 7, 121
community, WWE in the **184–5**
Corbin, Baron 78, 79, 164
Crews, Apollo 78, 137
cruiserweights **82–3**

## D

D-Generation X 13, 102–3, **106–7**, 135, 188
Dallas, Bo 166, 183
Del Rio, Alberto 68, 141
Demolition 19, 121, 127
DiBiase, Ted 7, 19, 21, 22, 37, 39, 139, 153, 183
Diesel 18, 87
Dillinger, Tye 160
*Diva Search* 190–91
Douglas, Shane 156, 157
The Dudley Boyz 96, **114–15**, 118, 157
Dudley, Bubba Ray 41, 98, 114–15, 118
Dudley, D-Von 114–15
Dudley, Spike 114, 157
Duggan, "Hacksaw" Jim 136, 194
Dusty Classic **172–3**

## E

ECW **156–7**
ECW Championship 100, 101
Edge 10, 35, 101, 118–19, 124, 140, 141, 142, 146, 150
Edge and Christian **118–19**, 180
*Elimination Chamber* 142–3
The Eliminators 115
Ellering, Paul 112, 117, 160, 172
Emma 60, 168, 187, 193
Epico 123
European Championship 101
Evolution 14, 37
*Extreme Rules* **150–51**

## F

fan base **194–5**
Flair, Charlotte see Charlotte
Flair, Ric 11, **14–15**, 30, 37, 61, 64, 74, 88, 94, 112, 113, 121, 137, 138, 144, 154, 169, 174, 194
Foley, Mick 48, **49**, 92, 93
The Four Horsemen 14, 15, 110, **112–13**, 154
Fox, Alicia 168, 187, 192
Full Sail University 161, 164
Funk, Terry 156, 157

## G

Gallows, Luke 96, 122
The Glamour Girls 101
The Godwinns 117
Goldberg 137, 144

The Golden Truth 123
Great Khali 77, 137, 148
Guerrero, Eddie 124, 125, 146, 148, 154
Guerrero, Vickie 101, 151

## H

Haku 7, 19
Hall, Scott 110–11
Hardcore Championship 100, 101
The Hardy Boyz 17, 114, 115, 118, 126
Hardy, Jeff 40, 88, 114, 118, 140, 147, 150, 153
Harlem Heat 110, 126
Harper, Luke 37, 79, 170
The Harris Brothers 126
Hart, Bret "Hit Man" 13, **28–9**, 31, 87, 94, 135, 136, 139, 146
The Hart Dynasty 109
The Hart Foundation 29
Hart, Owen 28
Hawk 19, **116–17**
The Headbangers 97, 124
Heenan, Bobby "The Brain" 19, 81, 120–21
The Heenan Family 19, **120–21**
*Hell in a Cell* **143**
Henry, Mark 77, 101, 108
Heyman, Paul **80**, 157
Hogan, Hulk 7, 8, 9, 10–11, 19, 38, 39, 66, 87, 110, 111, 121, 124, 139, 144, 146, 152, 153
Holly, Crash 98, 101
Honky Tonk Man 18, 19, 89, 147
Hornswoggle 49, 83, 151, 182

## I

Intercontinental Championship **88–9**
Iron Sheik 11, 98
Iron Team Tournament 117

## J

James, Mickie 17, 78, 91, 135, 146, 168
Jannetty, Marty 12, 19, 135
Jarrett, Jeff 56, 101
JBL 18, 35, 57, 139, 148, 181, 192
Jericho, Chris 4–5, 12, 43, **56–7**, 63, 69, 88, 98, 134, 135, 137, 142, 146, 148, 150–51

Jordan, Jason 125, 160
The Jumping Bomb Angels 101
Junkyard Dog 138, 188

## K

Kaitlyn 60, 190, 191
Kalisto 78, 79, 171
Kane 20, 37, 38, 39, 57, 72, 81, 109, 129, 141, 142, 146, 150, 181, 182
Kelly, Kelly 60, 194
Kendrick, Brian 83, 109, 125
Kennedy, Mr. 38, 140
Kidd, Tyson 96, 105, 186
*King of the Ring* **98–9**, 178
Kingston, Kofi 104, 105, 146, 181
Koloff, Nikita 95, 112
Kowalski, Killer 9

## L

Lana 54, 186, 187
Lawler, Jerry "The King" 130, 138
Layfield, John "Bradshaw" 131
Layla 60, 91, 190
Lee, AJ 60, 90, 190
The Legacy 37, 106
The Legion of Doom 19, **116–17**
Lesnar, Brock **40–41**, 50, 80, 86, 137, 139, 141, 143, 147, 148, 181
licensing **188–9**
Liger, Jushin "Thunder" 155, 165
Lita 16, 17, 126
London, Paul 109, 125
The Lucha Dragons 104, 170, 171
Luger, Lex 94, 95, 111, 112, 113, 136, 144
Lynch, Becky 70, **74–5**, 79, 84–5, 113, 148, 169

## M

McCool, Michelle 60, 91, 190
McMahon family **46–7**
McMahon, Mr. 12, 21, 30, 37, 46–7, 54, 67, 86, 107, 128, 137, 174, 188, 192, 194
McMahon, Shane 46–7, 101, 106, 107, 128, 149, 174
McMahon, Stephanie 37, 39, 46–7, 49, 90, 92, 93, 128, 185, 188

McMahon, Vince 106, 179
managers
  *RAW* 48, 49
  *SmackDown* 48, 49
  superstar 80–81
Mankind 49, 87, 124, 152
Marella, Santino 146, 151, 192
Martel, Rick 19, 146
Maryse 60, 65, 81, 186, 187, 190
Maven 137, 191
The Mega Powers 22
Melina 91, 124
merchandise **188–9**
Michaels, Shawn 4–5, **12–13**, 19, 28, 39, 87, 106, 107, 134, 135, 139, 143, 146, 149, 152, 153
Midnight Express 116, 117, 145
Million Dollar Man *see* DiBiase, Ted
Minnesota Wrecking Crew 126
The Miz 36, 42, 56, **64–5**, 68, 81, 96, 109, 137, 174, 183, 186
MNM 109, 124, 125
*Monday Night RAW* 178
*Monday Nitro* **154–5**
*Money in the Bank* **140–41**
Moon, Ember 161, 165
Morales, Pedro 18, 87
movies **182–3**
Muraco, Don 98, 156
MVP 52, 95
Mysterio, Rey 57, 98, 124, 125, 137, 141, 146, 148, 153

**N**

Nakamura, Shinsuke 161, 166, 167
Nakano, Bull 73, 90, 135
Naomi 75, 79, 183, 186, 187, 191
Nash, Kevin 110–11, 144, 154, 155
The Nasty Boys 117, 126
Natalya 60, 74, 79, 101, 151, 169, 186, 187
Neville 76, 99, 166, 171, 194
New Age Outlaws 97, 106, 109, 115, 118
The New Day 43, 96, 97, **104–5**, 109, 137, 174, 189
The New Wild Samoans 117
New World Order 25, 102–3, 106, **110–11**, 112, 195
Nexus Stable 147
NXT 49, **160–61**, 190–91

NXT Championship **166–7**
NXT Tag Team Championship **170–71**
*NXT TakeOver* specials **164–5**, 180
NXT Women's Championship **168–9**

**O**

One Man Gang 8, 136
O'Neil, Titus 76, 105, 191
Orton, Randy 35, **36–7**, 38, 40, 41, 141, 142, 143, 146, 147, 149, 153
Otunga, David 131, 191, 193
The Outsiders 111, 126
Owens, Kevin 52, **58–9**, 92, 135, 165, 181

**P**

Page, Diamond Dallas 30, 154, 155, 194
Paige 60, 75, 90, 168, 181, 187
Parker, CJ 54, 164, 165
Perfect, Mr. 19, 121
Performance Center **162–3**
Phoenix, Beth 60, 91, 137, 146, 194
Pillman, Brian 83, 112
Piper, Roddy 28, 145
Prime Time Players 104
Primo 123
Punk, CM 40, 57, 80, 86, 140, 143, 147, 150, 153, 156, 189

**Q**

The Quebecers 135

**R**

Race, Harley 30, 95, 138, 144, 154
Rae, Summer 168, 183, 187
Ranallo, Mauro 82, 131
Raven 95, 156
*RAW* **134–5**
  general managers 48, 49
  guest hosts 134
  superstars 76–7
  tag teams 122–3
  WWE Draft 174–5, 179
  WWE Universal Championship 93
Regal, William 49, 99, 149, 163, 169
Reigns, Roman 44, 51, 53, **54–5**,

59, 63, 92, 94, 129, 139, 141, 143, 149, 150, 152, 153
The Revival 164, 170
Rhodes, Cody 37, 89, 130
Rhodes, Dusty 112, 155, **172–3**
Rhyno 97, 119, 124, 148
Richter, Wendi 31, 90
The Road Warriors 112, 116, 117, 145, 160
Roberts, Jake "The Snake" 6–7, 39, 73
The Rock 11, **26–7**, 35, 38, 41, 86, 87, 106, 124, 137, 152, 153, 182
Rock 'n' Roll Express 126
The Rock 'n' Sock Collection 124
The Rockers 12, 19
Rogers, Buddy 8, 31, 86, 179
Rollins, Seth 37, **50–51**, 53, 56, 59, 72, 92, 95, 129, 139, 141, 153, 167
Roode, Bobby 160, 161, 167
Ross, Jim 130, 175
Rotten, Axel 157
Rotten, Ian 157
Rowan, Erick 27, 79
*Royal Rumble* **136–7**, 178, 194
Rude, Rick 81, 95, 121
Rusev 54, 76, 77, 174, 186
Ryback 53, 54, 66, 142, 150, 153
Ryder, Zack 65, 88

**S**

Sammartino, Bruno **8–9**, 31
Samoa Joe 161, 164, 166, 173
Santana, Tito 19, 22
Savage, Randy "Macho Man" 11, **22–3**, 73, 89, 111, 121, 132–3, 136, 138, 139, 144, 153, 154
Sensational Sherri 90, 146
Sheamus 52, 54, **62–3**, 96, 99, 139, 141, 151
The Shield 142, 153, 192
The Shining Stars 123
*Showdown at Shea* 178
Slater, Heath 97, 105, 124, 175, 183
*SmackDown Live* **148–9**
  general managers 48, 49
  superstars 78–9
  tag teams 124–5
  WWE Championship 93
  WWE Draft 174–5, 179
The Social Outcasts 123
*Starrcade* **144–5**

Stasiak, Shawn 153
Stasiak, Stan 87
Steamboat, Ricky 94, 126
The Steiner Brothers 112, 117, 126, 134, 135
Sting **24–5**, 106, 112, 129, 138, 144, 154, 155, 188
Stratus, Trish **16–17**
Strowman, Braun 76, 77
Studd, Big John 120, 121, 136, 139
Styles, AJ **42–3**, 50, 53, 87
*SummerSlam* **146–7**, 178
*Survivor Series* **152–3**, 178
Suzuki, Kenzo 125
Swann, Rich 83, 172
Sycho Sid 135, 152

**T**

*Tables, Ladders, and Chairs* **142–3**
Tag Team Championship **96–7**
Tamina 181, 187
Tazz 156, 157
Team B.A.D. and Blonde 187
Team Hell No 142, 192
Team WCW 111
Team WWE 147
Texas Tornado 19, 121
Titan Tower 179
TM-61 172
Torres, Eve 60, 190, 194
*Total Divas* **186–7**
*Tough Enough* 190–91
tours, international **192–3**
training **162–3**
*Tribute to the Troops* 178
Triple H 18, 20, 25, 37, 40, **44–5**, 47, 50, 56, 67, 87, 100, 106, 107, 128, 129, 130, 135, 138, 141, 142, 143, 144, 147, 152, 160, 161, 182
TV shows **180–81**, 186–7

**U**

Ultimate Warrior **18–19**, 25, 31, 89, 121, 132–3, 139, 147, 153, 188
Umaga 149, 192
Undertaker 6, 13, 28, **38–9**, 72, 80, 81, 87, 124, 134, 137, 140, 143, 146, 149, 152, 153, 174, 188, 191, 192
United States Championship **94–5**
Uso, Jey 108–9
Uso, Jimmy 108–9, 186

The Usos 97, **108–9**, 122, 125

**V**

Vader, Big Van 87, 144, 154
Valentine, Greg 19, 145
Van Dam, Rob 36, 41, 56, 125, 140, 156, 157
Vaudevillains 97, 123, 170
Von Rashke, Baron 117

**W**

WarGames 112
WCW **154–5**
WCW Tag Team Championship 126
Woods, Xavier 105, 114
World Heavyweight Championship 100
The World's Greatest Tag Team 109
*WrestleMania* 137, **138–9**, 178, 194, 195
WWE Championship **86–7**
WWE Divas Championship 90, 91, 101
WWE Draft **174–5**, 179
WWE Hall of Fame **30–31**
WWE Network **180–81**
WWE Studios **182–3**
WWE Universal Championship **92–3**
WWE Universe **194–5**
WWE Women's Championship **90–91**
WWE Women's Tag Team Championship 101
Wyatt, Bray 37, 72, 79, 108, 149
The Wyatt Family 27, 37, 109, 170

**X**

X-Pac 106, 118

**Y**

Yokozuna 134, 136, 139
Young, Darren 76, 191
Young, Renee 131, 186

**Z**

Zayn, Sami 76, 77, 88, 164, 165, 166, 167
Zbyszko, Larry 9, 112
Ziggler, Dolph 52, 56, 64, **68–9**, 81, 89, 101, 129, 141, 151, 181

**Senior Editors** Hannah Dolan and Tori Kosara
**Editors** Pamela Afram and Kath Hill
**Senior Designer** Nathan Martin
**Designers** Jaynan Spengler and Rhys Thomas
**Assistant Designer** James McKeag
**Pre-Production Producer** Marc Staples
**Producer** Sarah Burke
**Managing Editor** Paula Regan
**Managing Art Editor** Jo Connor
**Art Director** Lisa Lanzarini
**Publisher** Julie Ferris
**Publishing Director** Simon Beecroft

**Global Publishing Manager** Steve Pantaleo
**Vice President, North American Licensing** Jess Richardson
**Executive Vice President, Consumer Products** Casey Collins
**Photo department** Josh Tottenham, Frank Vitucci,
Georgiana Dallas, Jamie Nelson, Melissa Halladay,
Mike Moran, JD Sestito
**Vice President, Intellectual Property** Lauren Dienes-Middlen
**Senior Vice President, Creative Services** Stan Stanski
**Creative Director** John Jones
**Project Manager** Sara Vazquez

Dorling Kindersley would also like to thank Helen Peters for the index, Alex Beeden for
the proofread, and Dominic Aveiro, Joseph Stewart, Laura Palosuo, and Natalie Edwards
at DK for editorial assistance.

First American Edition, 2017
Published in the United States by DK Publishing
345 Hudson Street, New York, New York 10014

DK books are available at special discounts when purchased in bulk for sales
promotions, premiums, fund-raising, or educational use. For details, contact:
DK Publishing Special Markets, 345 Hudson Street, New York, New York 10014
SpecialSales@dk.com

Printed in China

A WORLD OF IDEAS:
**SEE ALL THERE IS TO KNOW**

www.wwe.com
www.dk.com